£1.99
4/4

GW01337539

# EASY STEPS TO NATURAL
# *Healing*

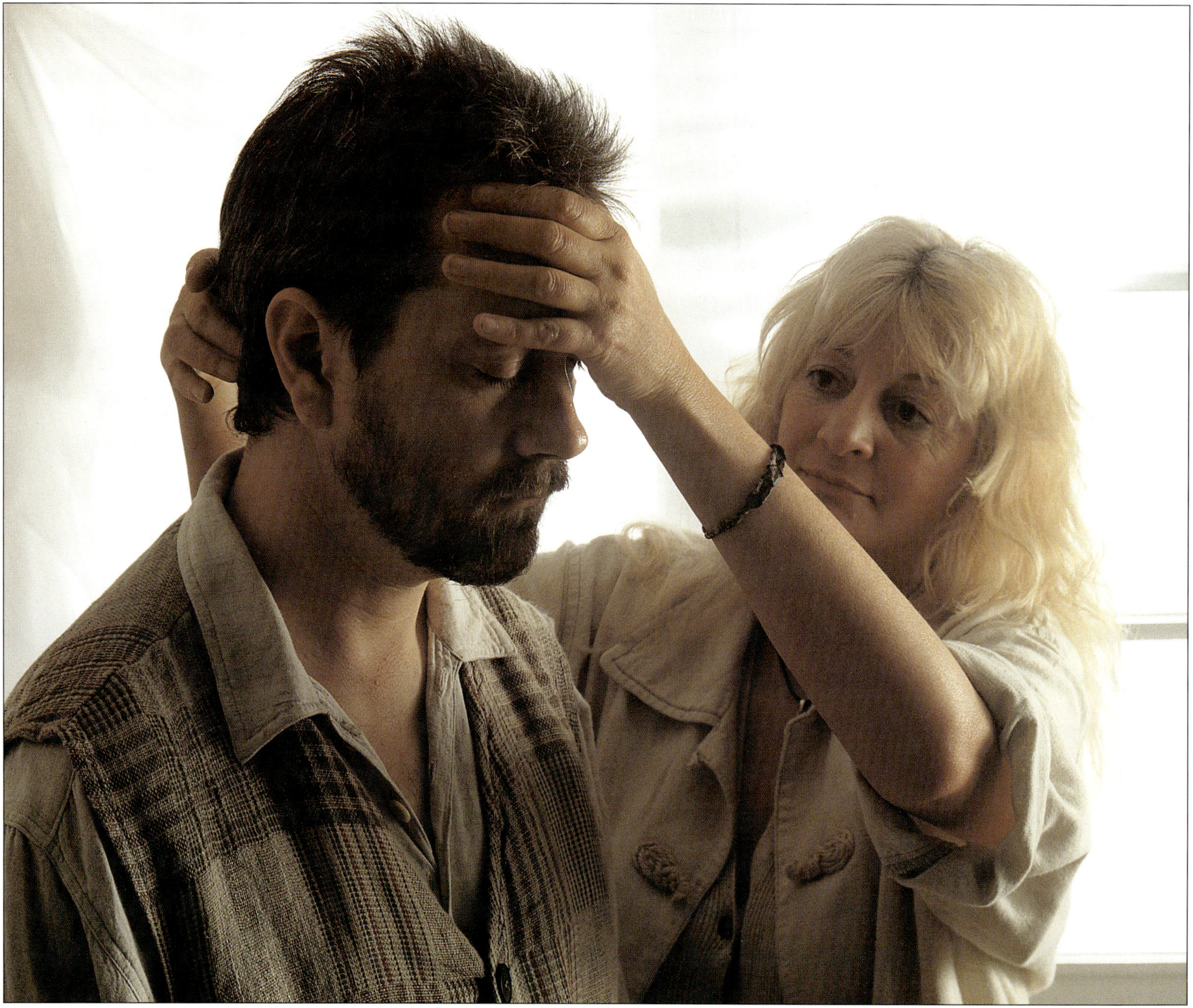

EASY STEPS TO NATURAL

# *Healing*

### Rosalind Widdowson

CAXTON EDITIONS

This Edition Published 2000 by
Caxton Editions an Imprint of
The Caxton Publishing Group

ISBN 1 84067 1084

All rights reserved. No part of this publication
may be reproduced, stored in a retrieval system, or
transmitted in any form or by any means, electronic,
mechanical, photocopying, recording or otherwise, without the
prior permission of the copyright holder.

*Printed in Hong Kong.*

## Special Thanks:

I would like to extend special thanks to my dear friend, Chrissie Coburn-Krzowska. She has been a fountain of knowledge and inspiration in the writing and compiling of this book. Her work as a healer was put to the test throughout the project. Like us, she went through the healing practices and processes, not just in the written sense but in the tried and tested one, real life.

We can all vouch for the validity of the methods and have no hesitation in recommending them. I'd also like to give special thanks to my partner, Stephen Marriott, who has been so patient and hard-working and my lifelong friend Pam Griffith, for her hard work in helping to present this work in such an attractive manner and Maria Clarke for her loving support, as always.

I dedicate this work to the memory of my dear friend and sister of the spirit, Carol.

Time is a great healer.
All that is past, is past.
There are many things in life we must experience
So we can step forward in Spirit.
It takes time to know this.

The dawn has to come,
Light to enlighten,
Rising like a bird from the gloom
To fill the eyes, the senses, the feelings,
With bright, glimmering understanding.

Dawn may last a thousand years
But it is always filling the Universe.
Everyone should seek the dawn and so be born again.

### Rosalind Widdowson

MBBO, IDTA, BWY, is a Natural Health Lifestyle Consultant. Her work and research have taken her all over the world and her pioneering spirit stems from a fascination with natural health and the environment. For 30 years she has taught in a refreshing and stimulating way and her deep-seated interests have enabled her to develop new and imaginative ways of teaching which have helped to establish her as one of the leading authorities in the world.

Her interest in dance, posture, yoga, meditation, natural healing, massage, diet and, indeed, all natural therapies was inspired by her childhood in Africa and led to her training as a classical dancer and teacher. Work on TV and radio started with general health and fitness programmes.

Her writing career began in 1981 with her best-seller, 'Yoga Made Easy'. Rosalind's busy work schedule involves running courses at her centres in England, India, Greece and the Caribbean. She runs her own unique teacher training course and has networks among some of the leading natural health organizations throughout the world.

### Chrissie S. Coburn-Krzowska

CGCI, BA, BA (Hons) doctorate of Naturopathy.
Member of the Natural Medicines Society.
Full Healer-Member of the National Federation of Spiritual Healers. Member of the World Federation of Healers.
Qualified in Reiki – Usui Shiko Ryoho System of Healing.
Trained as 'Avatar'.
Has been a natural healer since a child and a full-time professional for the last 12 years.
Worked extensively with Native American healers. Her Cherokee name is 'Ge-tsi-nv-si-dv'
('she who has been sent to us').
Co-Founder and Principal of Happy Home Primary School for Tibetan Refugees, Kathmandu, Nepal.
Director (TERA) Tibetan Education Relief Association.
Founder Friends of Happy Home (FHH).
U.K. Director of FOCUS Friends' of Children United to Save (in association with Russian International Foundation of New Science RIFNS) which is the organization behind direct help for people suffering the effects of Chernobyl.
Tutor of Taiji Quan, Qi Gong, Taiji Qi Gong for 15 years.
Studied in China, U.S.A. and Europe with many Chinese and Western masters.
Studied Hatha and Raja Yoga from the age of 12 years.
Has studied in various Tibetan Buddhist Centres in Nepal, India, Tibet and Europe for 16 years. Her Tibetan Buddhist dharma name is 'Karma Yeshe Khandro'.
Presently engaged in working in a Tibetan refugee centre in the Indian Himalayas as a healer and teacher of Taiji Qi Gong.

**Rosalind Widdowson**

**Chrissie S. Coburn-Krzowska**

# CONTENTS

Introduction ............................................. 7

Natural Health, Whatever Works ..................... 9

The Nature of Suffering ............................... 10
- *Guide to Preventing & Healing Burn-out*

The Healer-Patient Relationships ................... 12
- *Curing & Healing*

Cleansing & Protection .............................. 14

Healing Exercises in Nature ......................... 16
- *Standing Meditation Healing Practice*
- *Using the Breath*

Healing The Mind ...................................... 19
- *Relaxing/Stilling Your Mind*
- *Meditation to Aid Single-Pointed Attention*
- *The Relative & Ultimate View of the Mind*
- *The Power of Positive Thinking*
- *Assertiveness*
- *Mind Your Language*
- *Conversation Observation*
- *Accommodation rather than Compromise*

Healing Your Relationships ......................... 24
- *Relationships With Partners*
- *Heartache & Heartbreak*
- *Relationships With Children*
- *Relationships With Parents*
- *Co-Listening*

Healing Your Emotions ............................... 28

Healing Your Body .................................... 31

Healing Through Your Senses ....................... 32
- *Hearing*
- *Sight*
- *Touch*
- *Smell & Taste*
- *Ideal Food Combinations*

Herbal & Flower First Aid ........................... 38

Healing Your Environment .......................... 40

Exploring Your Subtle Healing Energies ........ 41

Healing Your Life ..................................... 42
- *Preparation of the Room*
- *Preparation of the Body*
- *Sitting Positions & Postures*
- *Sitting on a Chair*
- *Visualization*
- *Checking the Body Tension*
- *Stabilizing of the Breath*
- *Meditation on Giving and Receiving*
- *Meditation on Kindness*
- *Tong-Len Meditation*

Useful Addresses ..................................... 48

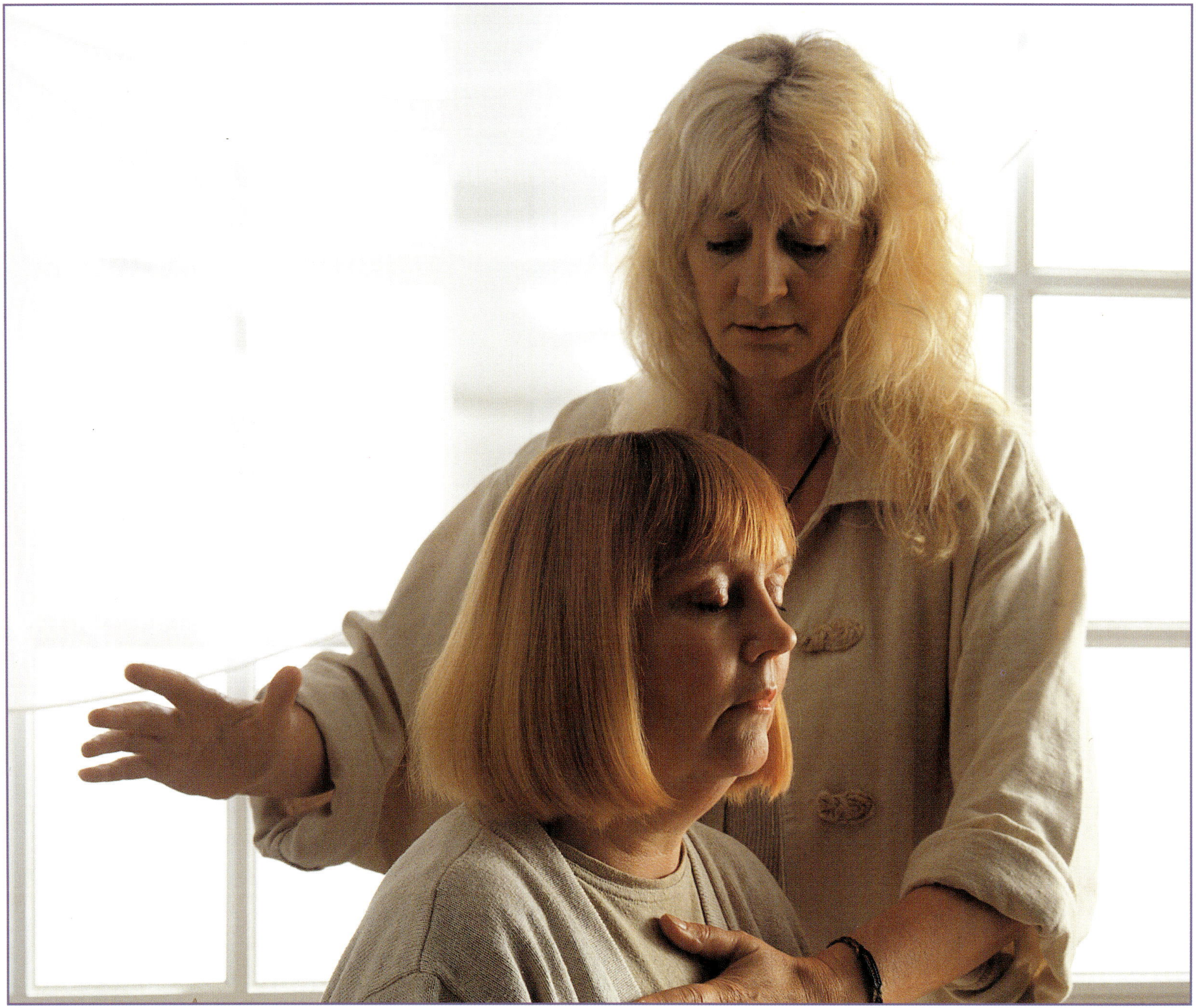

# INTRODUCTION

I have compiled 'Easy Steps to Natural Healing' with the help of my partner Stephen Marriott and our dear friend, Chrissie Coburn-Krzowska. She is an international healer, valued for her down-to-earth practical approach. We agreed right from the beginning that this book would not be dogmatic with repetitive dos and don'ts. The outline we felt would be most helpful to the novice was one that gave practical information.

We wanted to reflect the sense of freedom, free-will and fun which is a key part of our approach to life. This does not mean the book is without firm foundations for we have been involved with health and healing for many years. Our aim is to take the dogma and 'preciousness' out of healing, especially the myth that it can only be achieved by the expert practitioner. We hope you will be inspired to use the ideas as tools for your own processes and practices.

**"The best things in life are freed."**

Once you loosen up and start to look at basic ways of helping yourself and others, your whole philosophy of life will take on a new dimension. Most of us are struggling to find freedom in our lives in one form or another – freedom from too much work or too little work, illness, poverty, restrictive and unsatisfactory relationships, etc. What we are offering is a chance to enjoy, experience and experiment with ways in which you can lighten up and look at life with a broader vision.

We are offering a way to observe yourself and others in a new light. Not with a critical eye but rather a constructive one in which you can improve what you have rather than grieve over what you have not. It offers an opportunity to take a good look at the root causes of problems and why you have certain illnesses, then to work out an appropriate healing practice to suit your needs. The easy step-by-step format will help you to heal various aspects of your mind, body, emotions or spirit.

The curious part of writing this book is that the key players, including Pam Griffith our set designer, all had healing experiences either while being photographed with Chrissie or during the writing of the manuscript. If you persevere with these tried and tested practices, I can assure you that there will be a marked improvement in all aspects of your life.

This natural process involves removing the veils of ignorance or obstacles to our understanding of our true natural state. Therefore anything that comes in the way of our leading full, healthy, natural lives should be removed. True health comes from freedom and 'letting go' rather than 'acquiring' and 'burdening'.

Previous philosophies which tended to view the health of body and mind as separate issues, with little inter-connection between the two, have now turned full circle. Many people now realize that it is of the utmost importance to heal the 'whole person' rather than single aspects of the mind or body. Our attempts through alternative or complementary approaches, combined with the allopathic system in addition to the continuing growing interest in mind, body and spiritual techniques is leading to a 'holistic' approach towards health. In some cases it is leading to a more spiritually aware and enlightened end result. It is worthwhile pointing out that enlightenment is not just a case of 'seeing the light' but could be more helpfully viewed as becoming lighter rather than heavier, simpler rather than complicated.

The underlying thread running through this book is the nature of suffering itself. All too often we blame our environment, bad luck or other people for our own problems. Acknowledging our responsibility for our own part in all these things is the first step to the process of self-healing. This recognition empowers us to make appropriate changes for the better. If you believe that someone has the power to heal you, rather than the fact that the natural healing resources are awakened from within, an unnatural dependency on an outside source may arise. This is a process of disempowerment.

You may have noticed the paradoxical views we have just outlined. This is the nature of our 'dualistic reality'. Life is a paradox. The only constant we can be sure of is our capacity to change. In natural healing we seek to balance the apparent opposites. Often it takes a traumatic illness before we are prepared to change: suffering can be a great teacher and healer.

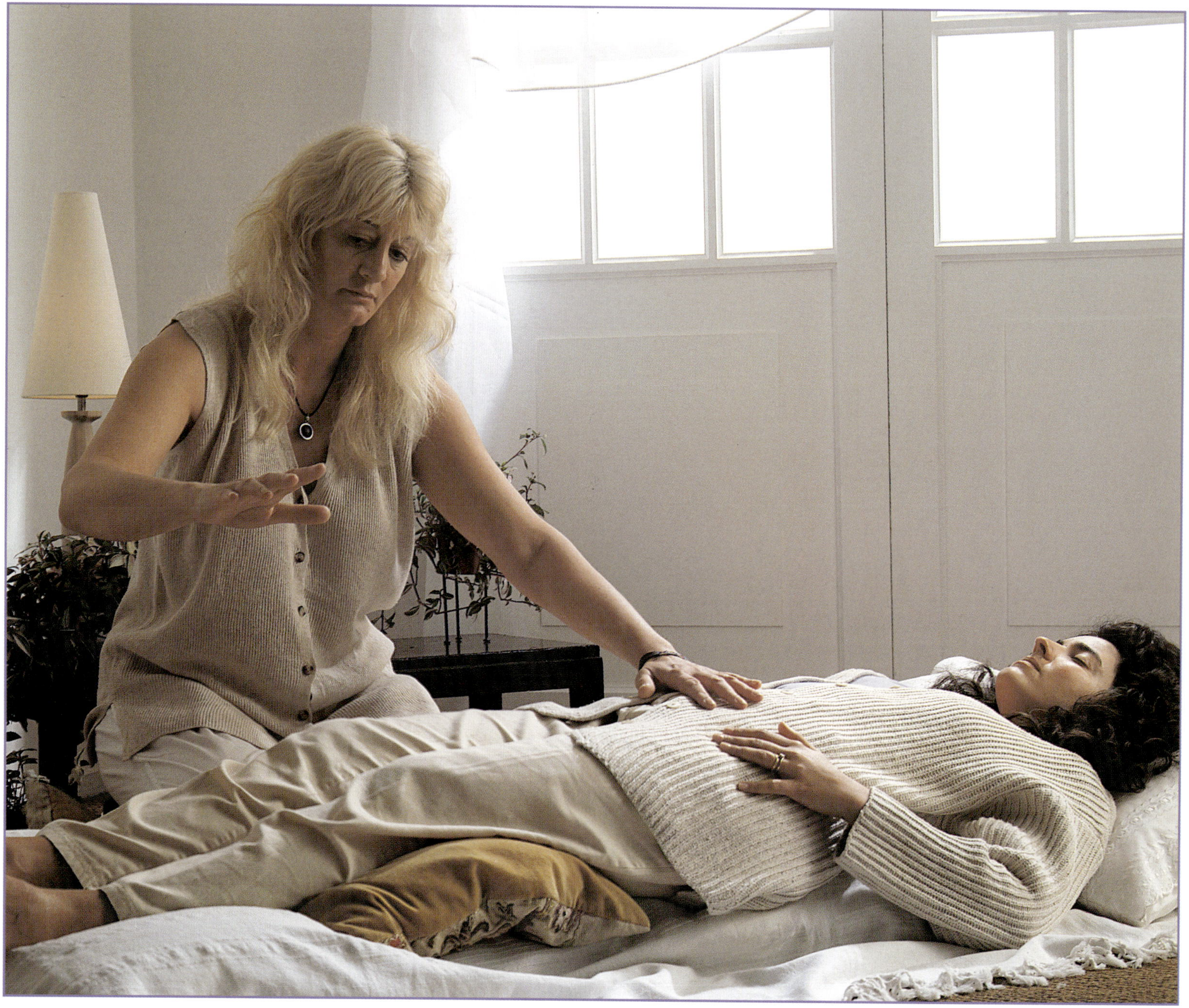

# NATURAL HEALTH, WHATEVER WORKS

Natural forces within us are the true healers of disease. Throughout history each culture has had its own model of what healing is and how to bring about its effect. Techniques vary according to cultural and personal beliefs. The phenomenon has been recorded in history for thousands of years, yet is still not fully understood.

What does healing mean? Healing means different things to different people, but basically it offers relief from pain and suffering. The ultimate healing comes only through transcending suffering through liberation/enlightenment.

There are a wide variety of methods and models to explain healing. For instance, cures can be effected through religious systems, voodoo, charismatic healing, channelling, shamanism, faith, psychic methods, psychotherapy, psychiatry, hypnotherapy, spiritual/spiritualist healing. There are also herbs, change of diet, touch, massage, allopathy, naturopathy, homeopathy, even divine intervention – the list is endless. These involve external intervention whereas other methods include learning a self-healing system such as prayer/meditation, yoga, Tai Chi, Qi Gong, self-acupressure, psychodrama etc. Obviously we can't include all the wonderful range of possibilities.

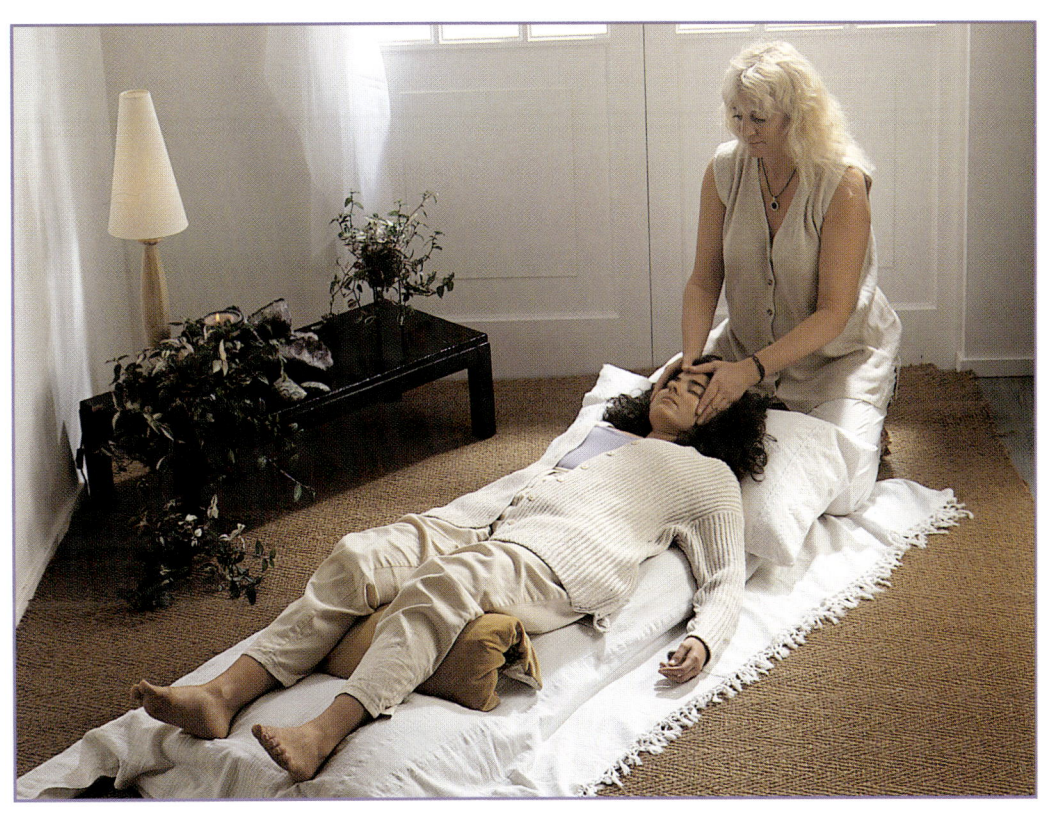

There is confusion between different methods, and attitudes towards the efficacy of natural healing vary with the differing degrees of confidence, ignorance, fascination, fear and faith which are attached to them. The techniques in this book are taken from various cultural/spiritual backgrounds. They have one common denominator, they are all humanistic systems and over long periods of time have been proved to be effective.

There needs to be a balance between naivety and keeping an open mind to the possibility that this form of healing might work. In other words, follow your natural instincts. Animals and children, for instance, respond positively to natural healing where faith is not a prerequisite.

The ideas we put forward in this book are tried and tested methods which have, simply, produced results. In the end, it's what works for you. So, keep an open mind and explore the endless possibilities that are available.

# THE NATURE OF SUFFERING

**"Suffering comes from within ourselves, it is an extension of our reaction to it."**

Suffering occurs when we try to resist pain, anger or any form of unpleasantness which we do not wish to accept into our lives. Instead of embracing and experiencing it, we resort to either anger or going into denial. This can only result in further suffering.

The action of pushing away (or holding onto) something we dislike, are activities that close us off from another area of experience, and exhaust our energies in the process. This creates exhaustion, pain and possibly disease, either mental or physical, with the result that even more suffering is created.

So where does suffering come from? We create it through ignorance of our true nature. Confusion arises in not understanding, and not wishing to make an effort to understand. We suffer when we have a sense of separation from what in our natural wisdom we know but may be incorrectly perceiving.

Suffering arises from attachment – attachment to people, places and experiences. When we become separated from any of these things we begin to suffer symptoms of withdrawal. This is why most suffering stems from our relationships with other people. We can become addicted to the idea that we cannot be happy without a certain person in our lives. If we become dependent on what is by its very nature impermanent, there will eventually be suffering. In other words, everything is transient, including ourselves.

To heal our suffering we need to understand our transitory nature. The essence of our enjoyment in experiencing a flower is that it, too, is ephemeral. The bud becomes a blossom, the petals fall and another stage in its cycle will develop. The seeds disperse and the cycle of renewal begins again.

If you look out in the world all around you there is suffering. Just as the Buddha said:
"... there is suffering; there's suffering of birth, there's suffering of old age, there's suffering of sickness and

*Buddha Menla – Medicine Buddha or the Buddha of Healing. A visualization tool to inspire or reawaken our innate buddha nature. Buddha is an awakened state of consciousness, not just a reference to the historical Buddha.*

*suffering of death"*.

There's suffering in getting what you want as well as what you do not want. There's even the suffering of getting what you want because, in time, it will change into something else and pass away. So, there is always fear associated with realizing your heart's desire.

Open your eyes and look around you, you will see suffering in so very many forms: sickness, illness, disease, poverty, hunger; physical, emotional and mental cruelty, fearful and battered children, imprisonment, torture, fear and violence – the list is endless. Even the people that 'make it' in an affluent culture suffer, only in different ways. Once wealth is accumulated or fame achieved there arises the anxiety of how to maintain or increase it.

If your human heart is open and full of empathy, it can be distressing to realize that there is nothing you can do to relieve that amount of suffering. The reaction of most people is to distance themselves with excuses such as: "I can't do anything about all that, so why should I try?" "It's other people's job to heal the sick, look after the old, defend the weak etc." "I've got to look after myself and my family first."

Even those who enter a caring profession for the altruistic reason of 'wanting to help', face the problem of 'burn-out'. If you regularly face the death and suffering of those you serve, come to know, and sometimes love, the whole thing becomes so painful you have to find an alternative. All too often carers seek protection from suffering by trying to become less involved and becoming 'professionally warm'. Those being cared for can instinctively recognize this attitude and the energetic interchange possible between healer and patient breaks down. Without that essential link, the value of care is greatly diminished. Indeed, true healing cannot occur without a committed and compassionate heart. This is the true dilemma for anyone who would perform a healing role – finding a balance between the wisdom where everything is the lawful working out of 'karma' (cause and effect) and the human heart that says, *"It's painful, I hurt."*

**There are many skills available for preventing and healing burn-out. Consider some of the following suggestions:**

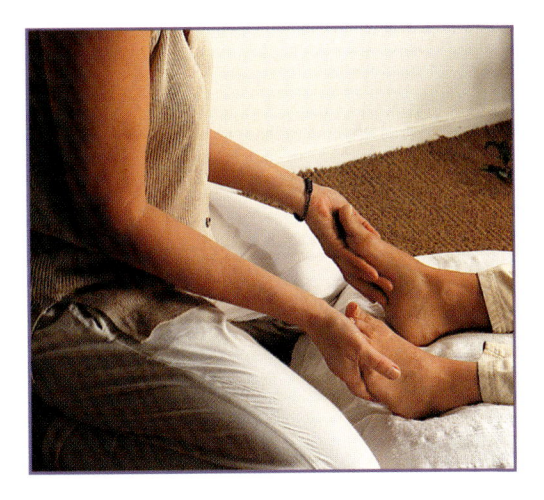

**Guide To Preventing & Healing Burn-Out**

- Reduce mental and physical stress with deep relaxation tapes or techniques, practise meditation, Tai Chi, Qi Gong, yoga, or some other personal development system.

- Seek support from a group or friend.

- Recognize your own limitations. Acknowledge your own needs and be kinder to yourself. Over-commitment can sow the seeds of future resentment.

- Forgive yourself for bouts of impatience or guilt. Having compassion for yourself will enable you to have compassion for others, (refer to Bach Flower Remedies, page 38, impatiens for impatience, pine for guilt).

- Take leave of absence for a while. Step outside your situation and 're-perceive' the problems you face. Even going out of the room for a few minutes and coming back again can produce a quite different perspective.

- Search for a deeper sense of who you are and discover how much more you have to offer without losing your own identity.

- Remain quiet and open to the light of your own truth, surrendering yourself to it rather than the darkness produced by martyrdom. Accepting what 'is' provides a space which opens us up to the potential for personal growth and understanding.

- Be conscious of how the seeds of burn-out start, by observing how you enter into a situation or decide to help someone.

- Misguided motives are the cause of many cases of burn-out. Only egotists surrender to pride by showing off how powerful, moral, worthy or efficient they are.

- Listen with your heart, be sensitive, and keep your feet firmly on the ground.

- Taking everything too seriously can leave you in danger of losing your own sense of lightness. So, if all else fails and you can't change the physical circumstances, try changing your attitude.

*"The deeper that sorrow carves into your being, the more joy you can contain!"*

# THE HEALER-PATIENT RELATIONSHIP

- The real skill of healing lies in the attitude. The healer accepts others as they are without making judgements but with a sense of deep compassion. They should respond to your individual needs in the most appropriate manner.

## CURING & HEALING

*"Even death can be a constituent of a healing if it occurs as a fulfilment in peace."*

Laura St. Aubyn

- There is a difference between curing and healing. You can be cured of the symptoms of a condition but unless the root cause is diagnosed and attended to, then you do not heal, you merely cause the problem to recur in some other line of least resistance. A cure may seem to have been effected in one place to emerge in another, whether it be in physical, mental or emotional form.

- Cures take place in different ways. A person may be healed spiritually yet not cured of the disease. One may still die, but in peace.

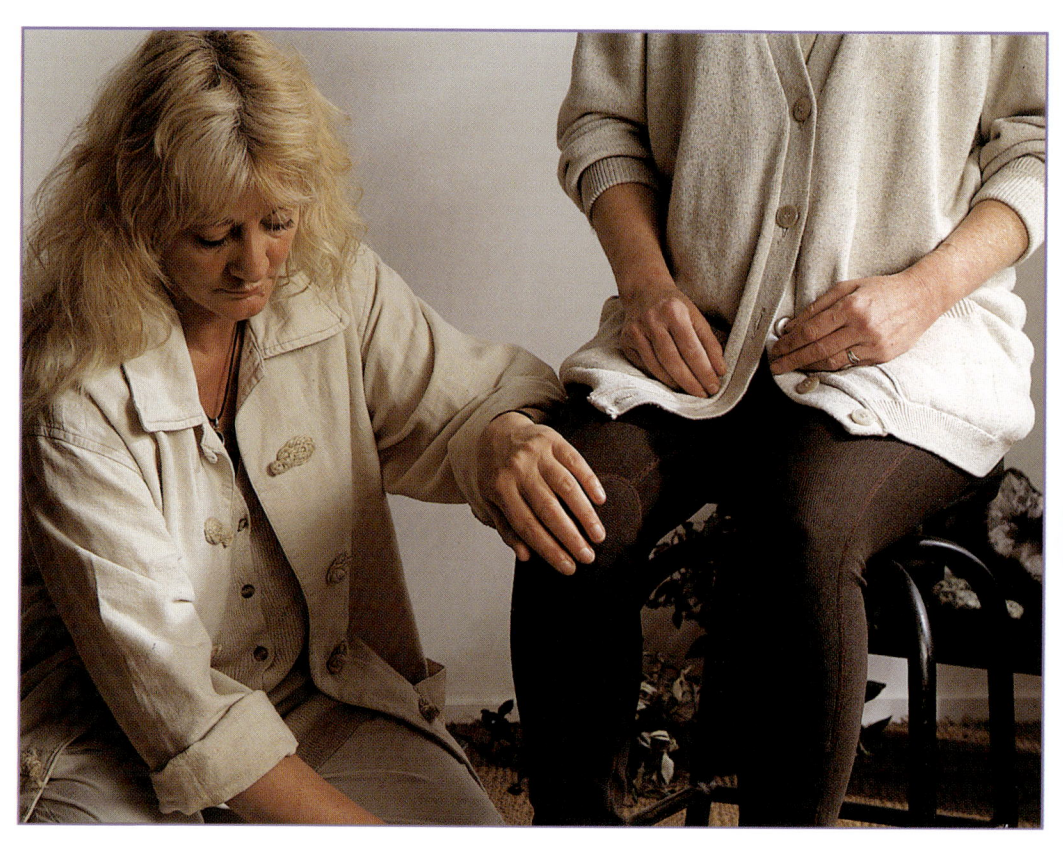

- There is a basic guideline which you might find useful when choosing a healer. Try to find a healer who is a member of a professional body, e.g. The National Federation of Healers: alternatively, one who has been personally recommended.

- In a healing situation, two people come together, by mutual consent, where the sense of separation or duality dissolves during the process. Then the roles of 'healer' and 'patient' disappear and a healing environment is created for their mutual benefit and not for the purpose of draining away the healer's energy. The role of the healer is no longer concentrated on 'giving' (channelling energy) and the recipient is no longer passively 'receiving'. Both enter a new dynamic of being present in a healthy and healing environment.

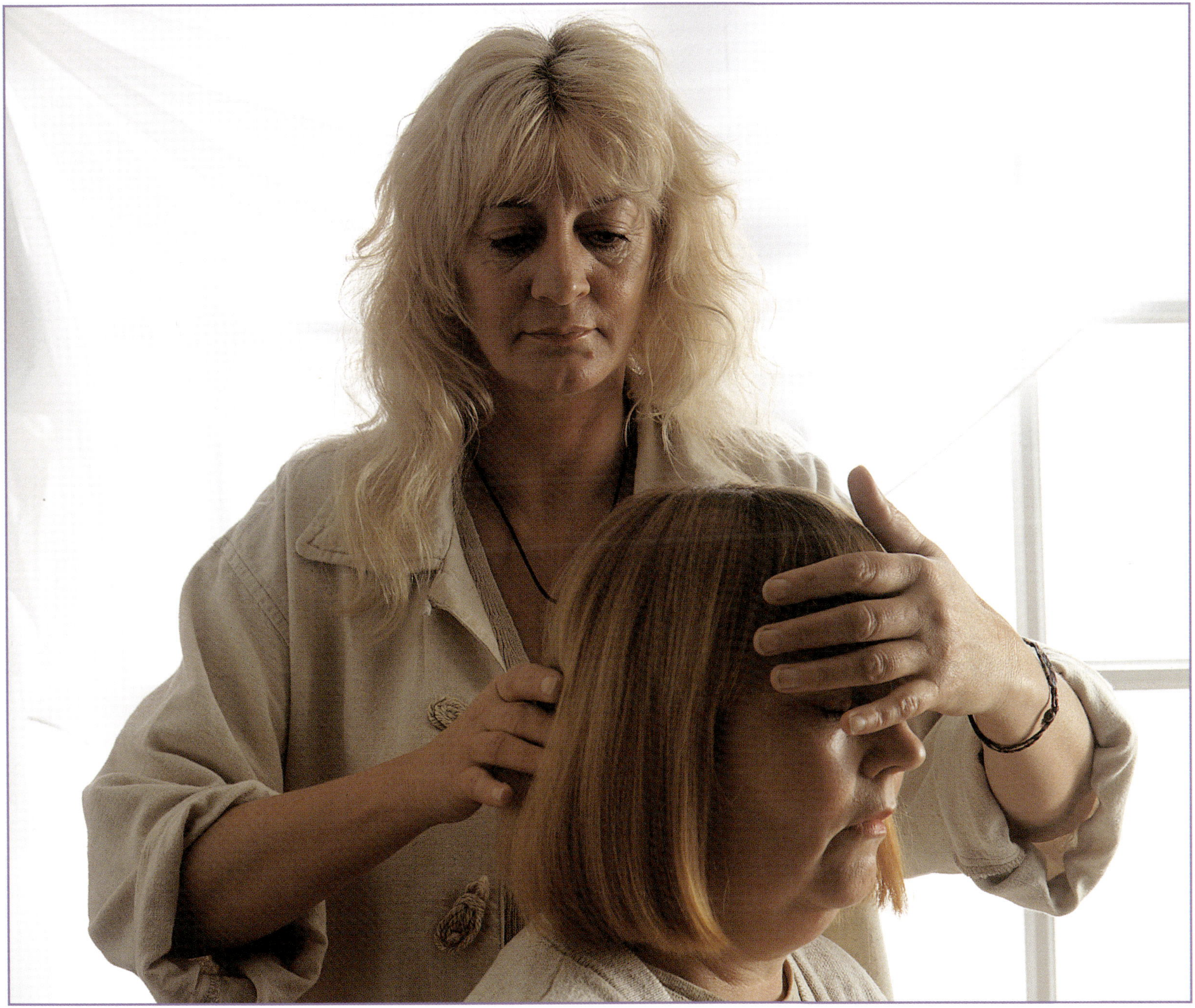

# CLEANSING & PROTECTION

These are rituals which allow us to clear our minds and bodies of any unhelpful associations or negatively-charged energies we may pick up, or inadvertently store from healing sessions. The following practices, rituals and routines can be performed at any time before, during or after a session – as and when the need arises. Remember, a trouble shared can be a trouble doubled!

## HEALING PRACTICE
### Cleansing

- Wash your hands in hot or cold water, depending on the ambience, though cold is best for its refreshing quality.

- Use a crystal (amethyst) to absorb the negative energies.

- Perform a ritual act signifying the completion of an act of healing.

- Walk and take a breath of energizing fresh air.

- Have a natural pause or space.

- Shake your hands and feet and flick away the tension or negatively-charged energy, cold or sick Chi.

- Change your clothes (if necessary).

- Have a cup of tea, cold water or fruit juice following emotional discharge. Use Crab Apple (Bach Flower Remedy) either internally (drink) or externally (bath).

- Shower or bathe or visualize standing under a waterfall, purifying both outer body and inner being/meridians.

- Adopt the technique of 'smudging' burning sweet grass or sage which smoulders like incense. It is performed as a purification by the Native Americans. It is often used with an eagle's feather, wafting sweet-smelling smoke to purify either the person or the room. Incense can be used in a similar manner.

One of the most frequently asked questions in connection with healing is, "How do I protect myself?" If you are looking for a healer, go by personal recommendation and to someone who is a member of a recognized body such as the National Federation of Spiritual Healers, World Federation of Healing or the relevant schools of professional practitioners related to the chosen discipline, i.e. osteopathy, acupuncture, herbalism, etc. They will be governed by a code of practice and may also be protected both legally and financially.

While exploring healing for yourself, either as practitioner or recipient, the following practices and views may offer some guidance or framework of reference you may find useful. Bear in mind that, at its most profound, the viewpoint is that 'love protects all'. However, should you wish to combine ideas of protection with your religion or belief structure, this may give you the reassurance that can keep your mind open and assist the flow of healing energy.

**Note:** Attending to our physical body's protection strengthens the immune system which protects us against internal and external bacteria and viruses etc. When the body is out of balance, for example, it enables viruses, bacteria or fungi already present to increase, causing a physical manifestation of disease.

## HEALING PRACTICE
### Protection

- Lavender oil.

- Placing copper coin on navel.

- Make offerings or invocations within your chosen belief system, e.g. ask for protection from a deity or give healing in the name of Christ, the Father, the Holy Spirit, Allah, Buddha, Krishna, Rama, Shiva, Wakan Tanka (the Great Spirit). Use mantras (sacred sounds), recitation of the Lord's Prayer or take refuge in the Buddha or other reminders of the sacredness of all life.

- Use forms of meditation formulated for the purification of the mind. However, the greatest protector is motivation.

- Let common sense prevail. If there is anything which leaves you feeling uncomfortable, or feels unnatural, leave it alone and find some other way.

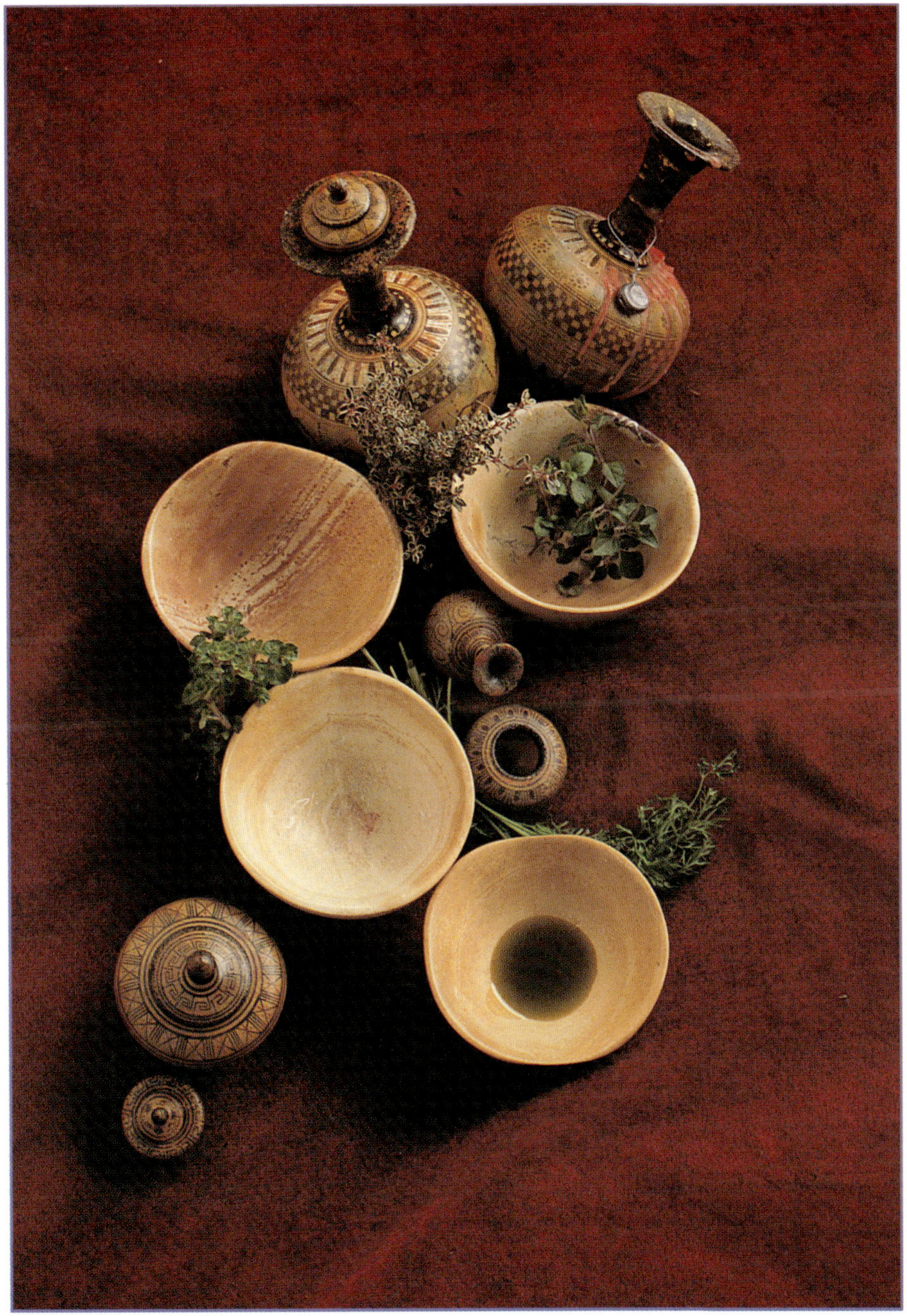

# HEALING EXERCISES IN NATURE

**"The higher you reach towards the heavens, the deeper your roots must be."**
*Chinese aphorism*

The wisdom needed to recognize your health problems is within you, waiting for you to be aware of it. All you need to do is bring it to the surface. Fear is your only enemy and love your best friend. The love of nature and connection with its energies can be felt by hugging a tree or walking in a beautiful forest. Bismarck, the German statesman, was advised by his physician to sit with his spine against a large oak tree, which was reputed to have healed his migraines.

Writings on the Taoist view of health and the cultivation of Chi (intrinsic energy), date back to the time of the Yellow Emperor (2690 B.C.) These relate to the Chinese view of the relationship between heaven, earth and humankind. The exercises formulated at this time were developed from a way of taking inspiration from nature.

The following simple standing meditation is common to Tai Chi Ch'uan (Taiji Q'uan) and Chi Gong (Qi Gong). The fundamental stance, together with its visualization and breathing method, can be used as a practice in its own right. It teaches us to be grounded and to explore the connection between earth and heaven (as expressed in the principles of Yin-feminine and Yang-masculine). Good health requires a balance between Yin and Yang forces in the body. On a larger scale, heaven is Yang whilst earth is Yin.

Most people are familiar with the above symbol. It is called Tai Chi – the 'Supreme Ultimate Principle of the Universe'. It illustrates the continual flow and play of complementary opposites. Yin contains the seed of its opposite, Yang, and vice versa. In the diagram, the circle is 'the One'. Within it is contained the quality of 'duality', their relationship is the third stage of transformation. Chi is generated from the interplay of the energy that binds these two qualities. With the following practice it is possible, in a simple way, to experience the flow of these two dynamic forces.

### Standing Meditation Healing Practice

- To begin, stand with your knees slightly bent, weight distributed evenly on both feet which are positioned directly below the shoulders. Stand with the feet parallel (hip or shoulder-width apart) on a natural surface such as earth or grass (but not concrete).

- Let your arms hang relaxed by your sides. Keep the spine straight but not rigid. This visualization is useful in correcting all kinds of back problems.

Concentrate on the crown of the head (bai hui). Imagine the skull being suspended by a cord, pulling the body upwards. Imagine the vertebrae as beads on a silken thread, hanging downwards. Experience the fluidity of the movement of the spine from such a viewpoint. On the in-breath, stretch the body upwards, 'opening the bones' of the spine, and on the out-breath relax the body without compromising the integrity of the stance. This practice alone is an excellent method for correcting and healing body posture.

- With knees relaxed, lean your weight slightly forward. Feel the contact with the 'bubbling spring' (yung-ch'uan), i.e. a point on the centre of the ball of the foot. Concentrate your weight on this area in order to open it out and allow the energy flow to and from the earth.

- Release all body tensions, from the scalp to the soles of your feet, by imagining them as ice crystals. Concentrate the mind slowly down the body, warming and melting the ice and allowing it to drain out through the 'bubbling spring' to discharge into the earth. Repeat three times.
  Imagine your energy extending from the 'bubbling spring' down into the earth like the roots of a tree.

- Then, keeping your feet rooted to the ground (Yin), drawing the earth's energy up slowly through the body, discharge any mental tension through the crown of the head into the sky above. Repeat three times.

### Using the Breath

Traditionally, in relationship to Qi Gong practices, exhalation is Yang, inhalation is Yin. Exhalation expels, discharges, releases. Inhalation brings in, gathers and collects.

As the Chinese classics say: "Expel the old, take in the new." After dispelling tensions we now re-energize the body. Locate the area known as the T'antien (Field of Immortality), by measuring three fingers below the navel, and imagining a line extending backwards just in front of the spine. This is the physical centre of movement and also the centre of Chi energy.

On the in-breath, draw fresh energy from the earth into this area. On the out-breath, discharge any mental tension, again through the crown of the head into the sky. Let the mind expand into the heavens to have a taste of the infinite. Rest in this space. When ready, on the in-breath, draw the fresh Yang energy down through the body and focus into the T'antien. On the out-breath, discharge any tensions, physical or emotional, downwards as far into the earth as you can conceive. Rest in this experience.

Repeat the procedures several times until you are happy with the feeling of balance between Yin and Yang energies. Finally, bring your mind to rest into the T'antien, to enjoy the sense of freedom and balance of your own centre of being. Experience the truth of your relationship with the earth you stand on and the universe around you. These practices will harmonize the relationship of the body and spirit through the use of the mind, and increase your awareness of the environment in which we live.

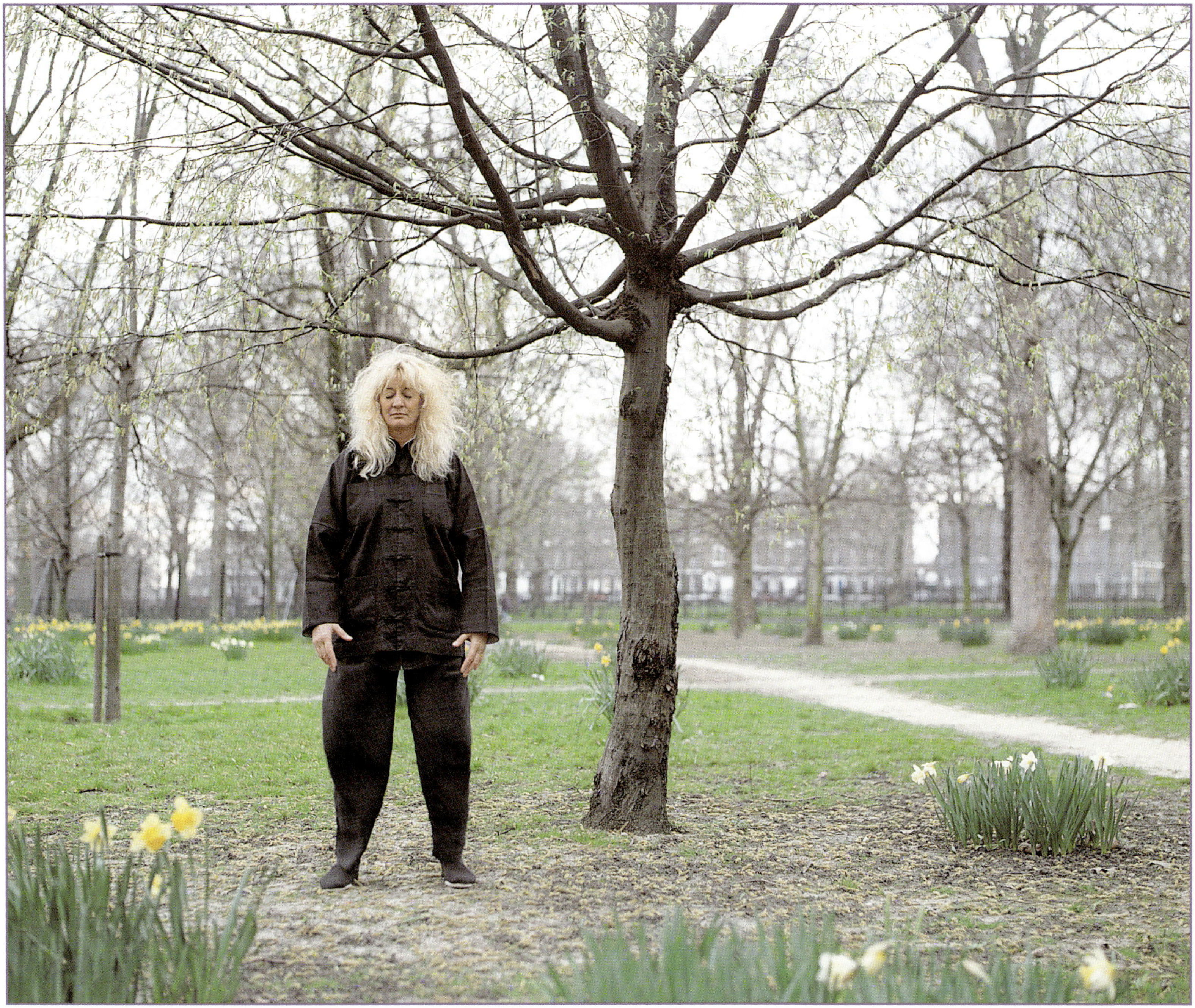

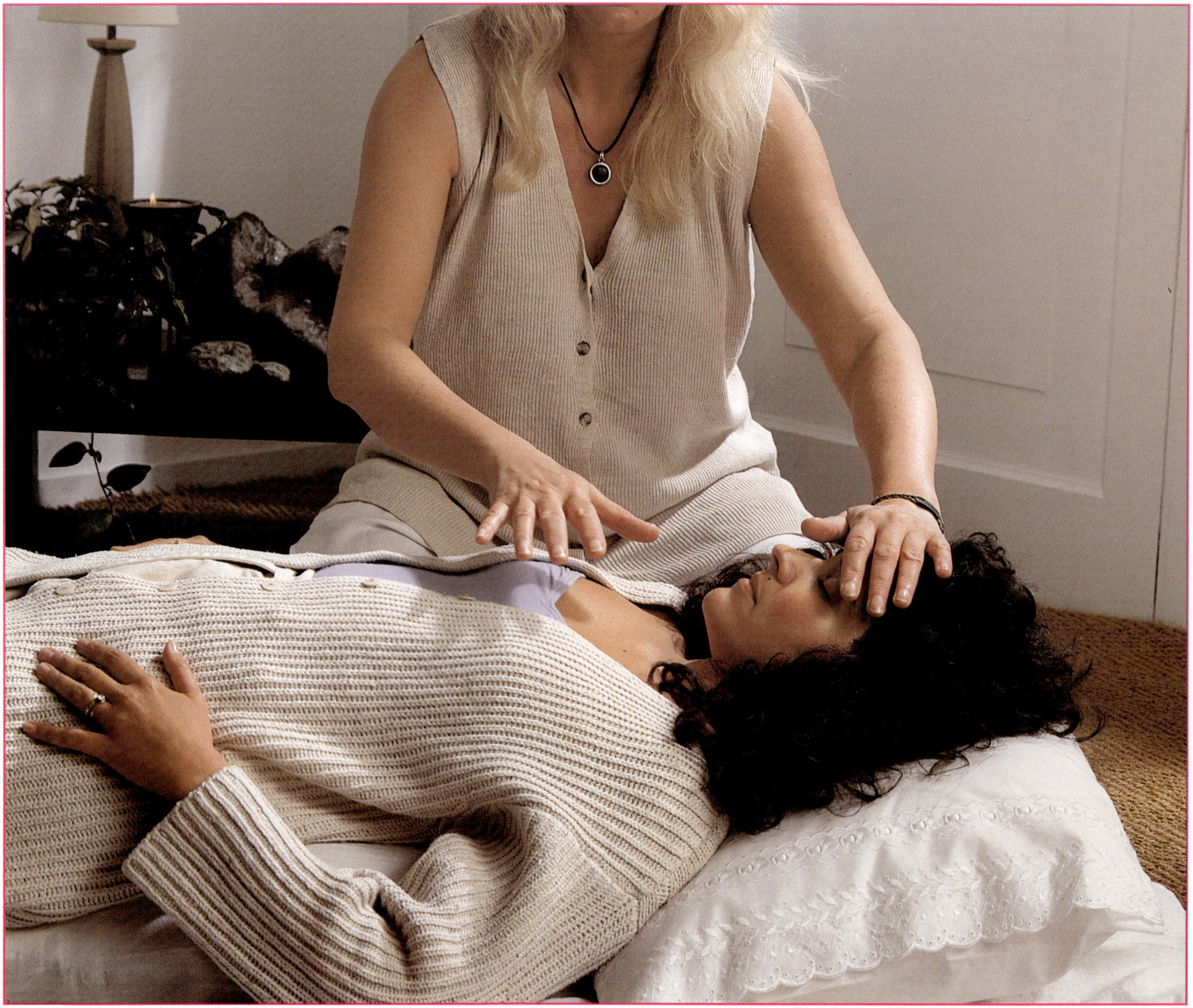

# HEALING THE MIND

> "Mind is the essence of everything.
> Due to the mind's purity, all becomes pure.
> Due to mind's clarity, all becomes clear.
> Due to mind's well-being, all becomes well.
> The essence of everything is one's own mind."
>
> Relative World, Ultimate Mind.
> The Twelfth Tai Situpa

Mind sets affect our health and if we do not service our whole selves, including our minds, how are we to be of help to other people? The whole purpose of a healthy body is to use it as a vehicle to understanding the mind. There is a saying in China which encompasses this thought: "The higher you reach towards the heavens, the deeper your roots must be." This is a good description of the relationship between the mind and the body. It is pointless concerning ourselves with 'mind matters' if our poor bodies are being neglected.

The first question I am likely to ask a client is "How are your plants doing at home?" If they are neglected or non-existent this gives me a practical insight and starting point from which to work. I usually ask them to start nurturing their plants, feeling the soil to see if extra water is needed, changing the plants' positions if they are not thriving. In other words, to maintain close contact with a changing, living thing. This may sound trivial, but in the majority of cases when the client no longer needs to visit me, their plants will have started to thrive. One girl told me her boy friend tried to persuade her to stop bringing plants home as he was beginning to feel he was living in a jungle. This mirrored how she had changed her life and gained interest in a new and rewarding project.

The mind accumulates all the sensory information it receives and works out what to do with it. We tend to think that the more information we feed into it the more knowledge, clarity and understanding we will have about life; but when it boils down to it, in order to assimilate information, we need to be quiet and allow the mind to rest in order for a natural spontaneous reaction to occur. That's where intuition comes in, which is considered by many to be the sixth sense. What we are doing, in fact, is tuning in to the male and female sides of our natures.

The male principle is concerned with the gathering in of knowledge and the creating of a foundation or framework. The female principle nurtures that knowledge allowing it to grow naturally and spontaneously. In other words, we do not have to coax our minds into using information, it is a natural process. The mind is able to receive information while at the same time creating space for things to happen and develop. We all have a mind of our own and we can so easily forget that fact. There is no need to distance ourselves from life's decisions, we do play an important part in the general pattern of things. Adhering to the old idea that God helps those who help themselves can be very useful in listening to, and acting on, our innermost thoughts. This can only occur if we create spaces within the mind to encourage thoughts to develop, for although the mind naturally functions on its own, we can allow our negative outlook to crowd our inner vision.

Meditation is an excellent way of helping to create that space within the mind. It is not about emptying the mind, but merely about observing in order to create space from our problems so that we can come back to them refreshed and inspired to look at them in a different light. Our perception of life, the world, the universe, is a reflection of our state of mind which is why something as simple as getting in touch with the part of the body that is distressed can actually give us energy by informing the mind of what is happening. In the same way we could just sit in silence and not do anything but be aware of what is taking place and the changes that are occurring. You can actually see, feel and experience changes just by being in a state of stillness. The wonderful thing is that the mind does not need any complicated instructions or scientific explanations to be able to help you. Meditation is an ancient art that allows the mind to balance on a fine line between total awareness and total relaxation.

Techniques vary according to the numerous states of mind in which we find ourselves. Here are a few starting exercises:

**Relaxing/Stilling Your Mind**

1. Sit in a comfortable chair, i.e. the 'postural chair' (the kneeling-style chair – as illustrated on page 43) is ideal for a comfortable starting position.

2. If your mind is agitated, keep your eyes closed or if your mind is dull and apathetic open your eyes and use a simple object on which to focus your attention. Choose a natural object such as a pebble, twig, shell or candle flame.

3. With eyes closed, concentrate on your breathing (through your nose). There is no need to alter it or adopt specific breathing patterns, just breathe naturally, being aware of what is happening, and see how certain thoughts make the breath go faster while other thoughts make the breath slow, deep and rhythmical.

4. Practise just being in the moment and savouring it.

**Meditation to Aid Single-Pointed Attention**

Patanjali, the yoga sage, called this technique, 'fixed attention'. The only requirement is to look and continue to look and when the attention wanders, gently guide yourself back to looking.

- Observe your need to constantly change your posture, perception and way of looking. You or the object may appear bigger, smaller, lighter, have energy haloes, etc. Keep on looking!

- Sometimes inspiring, sometimes rewarding, a ten-minute meditation with the same object every day will open up another level of understanding of your untamed mind.

*"... in the moments of stability
it is possible to have a glimpse of the beauty of
the peaceful radiance of
the natural mind through the chaos of
the conditioned mind's neurotic play."*

Chrissie Coburn-Krzowska

### The Relative and Ultimate View of the Mind

Most people become upset when they feel they cannot realize the expectations they have set for themselves. When they recognize their limitations and problems they can easily develop negative feelings. This can cause anger and depression. However, it is useful to know one's faults. Even though we suffer from the knowledge of our own mortality, it is important to appreciate that feelings of negativity do not last forever. This is our dualistic or 'relative' view.

### The Power of Positive Thinking

A positive outlook that is used and practised in your daily actions is one sure way of being able to reverse the grip of many diseases or illnesses. It offers you the chance to practise what you think and feel. You can devote as much time as you deem necessary but obviously the more regularly you practise, the more proficient you will become.

The way to begin is to take an honest look at the negative programming you have absorbed, e.g. you may be harbouring resentment or anger. At first, it may be difficult to acknowledge these aspects that lie within yourself as we all have the ability to turn a blind eye to certain aspects of our own character. Once you have ascertained where the weak or negative aspects of your personality lie, you can start to heal yourself by learning to positively forgive yourself. Learning to forgive yourself and others is a key step along the important path to self-discovery.

This is one of the main reasons why we become entrenched in negative thinking and 'living' in the future. The main point of power is in the now, the present moment. It is all too easy to swing like a pendulum between grasping at the future and wallowing in the past. This is a breeding ground for disappointment and self-pity.

The good news is that no matter how deep-seated these old habits are, you can begin to make a change right now. What you choose to say and think now will create your future. All you are in fact doing is returning to your original pure self. Previously, you have allowed life's experiences to cloud your outlook and by peeling back the layers you will be able to return to the truth of your being. Early programming by our parents and environmental influences have a lot to do with the way we view the world. Life's experiences do mirror our beliefs and actions. If you wish to have a rewarding and fulfilling life then you need to cultivate constructive and joyful thoughts.

Once you realize that the saying "As you think, so shall you feel" has the ring of truth then you can start to take full responsibility for your own life and stop blaming other people for what is happening to you. It won't be long before you notice that the everyday aches and pains that are wearing you down, such as headaches, migraines, muscular tension, were being caused by your inflexible negative outlook.

Positive thinking or affirmations may simply overlay old programmed patterns of thinking. In order to prevent this, enlist the help of a friend who is willing and able to make you fully aware of your own doubts, fears or other negative attitudes. They can do this by observing and providing feedback where your involuntry movements, change of facial expression and body posture, tone of voice (i.e. questioning or despairing), are concerned. The very act of recognizing these traits and letting them discharge will clear the mind of contradictions. Gradually, the truth of your affirmations will emerge and they will have the ring of authority and truth. Otherwise, all we do is increase our suffering by supressing genuine emotions such as doubt and fear by not allowing them expression. Ultimately, you are seeking the marriage of rational approach with the sensitivity to discharge the underlying feelings. The intellect has to engage in the experience of feelings and emotions (head and heart) – intelligence (intellect) with heart (not sentiment).

### Healing Practice

There are some simple rules to follow when constructing your personalized positive thought, your affirmation, resolution or Sankalpa (from the yoga tradition).

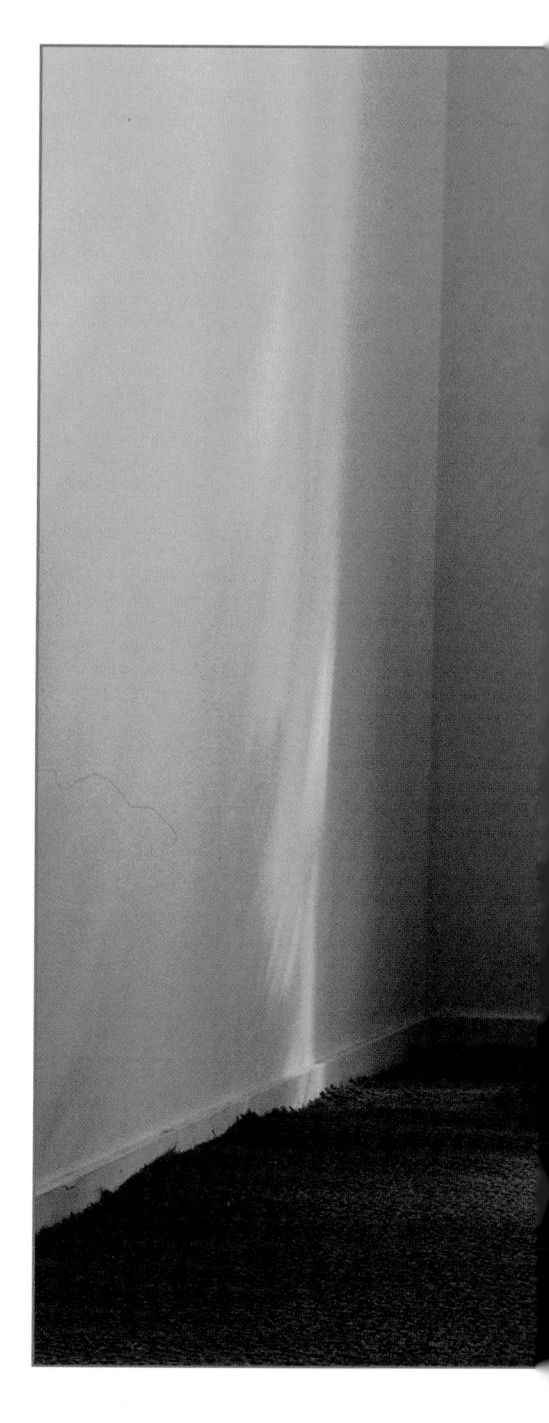

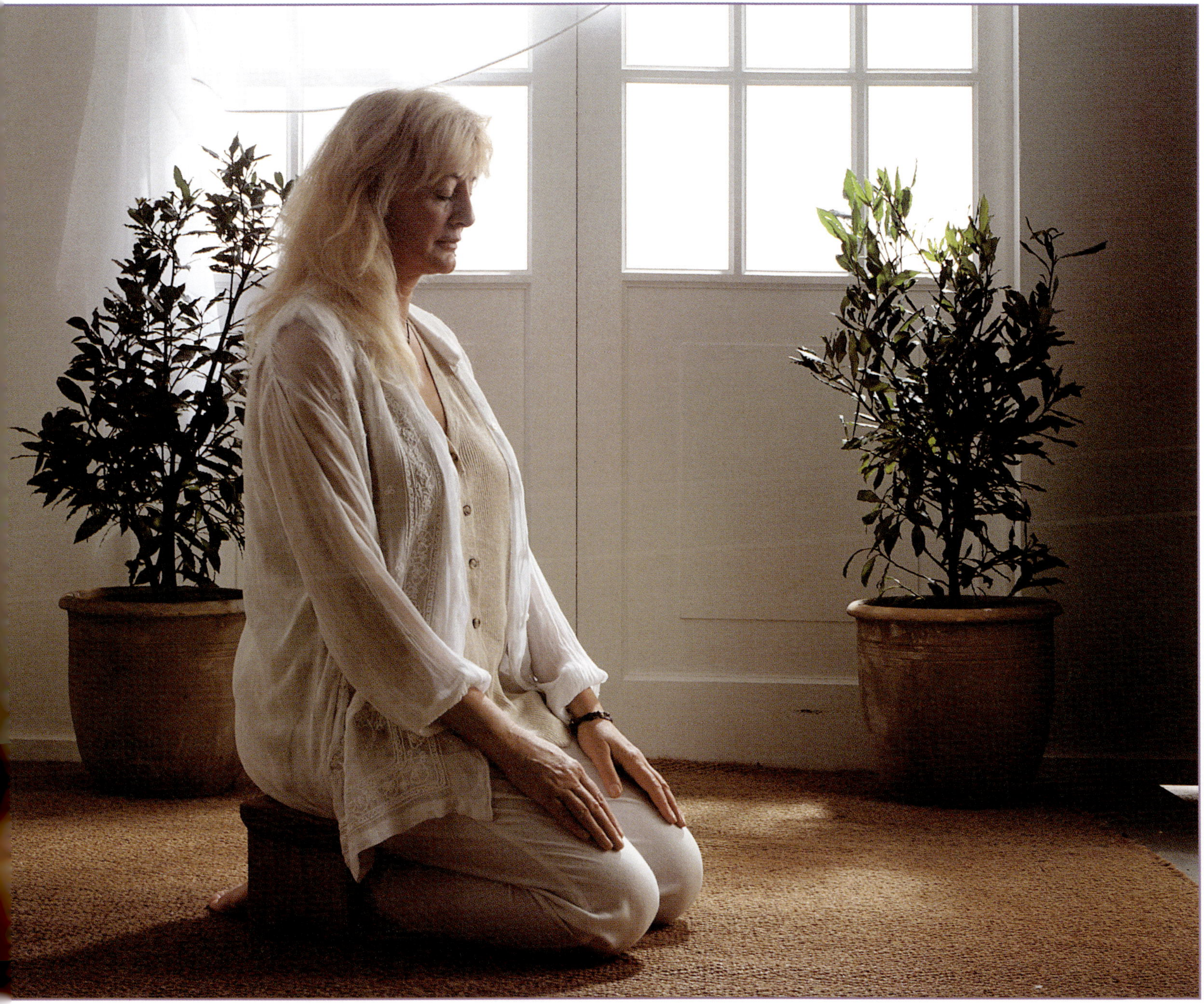

1. Firstly, define what you perceive as a negative trait or aspect of your life that is not working for you or is making you unhappy, e.g. "I am scared of meeting new people', "I'm fat", "I have no confidence", "I don't like myself", etc.

2. Turn these phrases on their heads, substituting words such as, "I am", "I can", "I will", and expressing them in a positive way. It may help to think of a person who has attributes you admire and imagine how they would make these positive assertions about themselves, e.g. "I enjoy meeting new people", "I am brimming with confidence", "My body is in the process of a change for the better". Ensure the phrase is short and pithy – too long and it will be difficult to remember or will not run off the tongue.

3. Be specific about the subject matter you choose. You should be able to monitor its effectiveness over the short to medium term. Wanting to love all the world all the time is somewhat unrealistic since you are unlikely to see the results of it in this lifetime and would not be likely to receive the encouragement to continue with this excellent technique.

4. Do not be discouraged if at first you do not believe what you are saying. Many beginners actually find it hard to articulate, even in the privacy of their own home.

### Healing Practice: Assertiveness

1. I am not on call to everyone, all the time.

2. I have needs of my own which may not be the same as my family, colleagues or friends.

3. I do not have to agree to every request that is made of me.

4. I don't have to carry on doing something just because I have always done it.

5. Time relaxing is well spent.

6. There is no such thing as the perfect wife, husband, mother, father, child.

7. Time spent feeling guilty could be spent doing more enjoyable things.

8. I won't always do things for others if they are capable of doing them for themselves.

9. I shall give myself the same care and consideration that I give to others.

10. I will remember, at all times, especially in the face of criticism, difficulties and anxiety, that 'I Am Doing The Best I Can'.

### Healing Practice: Mind Your Language

*"Argue for your limitations and you get to keep them."*

Our language reflects our thinking and feeling processes and our processes affect our language. If your language regularly contains the words:

a) 'can't', 'won't', etc., don't be surprised if a self-fulfilling prophecy establishes itself!

b) 'shouldn't' suggests you are stuck in your energy and find it difficult or impossible to accept another way of seeing.

c) 'right/wrong', 'good/bad', you are making a judgement. You are stating your own narrow view and showing inflexibility towards the possible range of views you might take that could expand your mind and enrich your life.

d) 'believe', you are limiting your experience to what you are prepared to see. To believe something you must 'not believe' a range of other possible alternatives. Your world will simply reflect the way you choose to see things. Try replacing limiting words with alternatives such as 'helpful', 'appropriate', 'apt'.

Have you ever observed two people having a conversation in a pub? Often it will start out with one person talking and the other listening. There will be a brief pause and the other will respond/reply. Within a couple of exchanges you may notice that the pause between speakers gets shorter and shorter. Especially if the subject is contentious (politics, sport, sex etc.), you will observe that the participants start formulating their response while the other is talking and the moment they finish start talking themselves. If the debate becomes still more heated, voices raise in volume and pitch and start to overlap.

### Healing Practice: Conversation Observation

a) Have a conversation with a friend about something you care about and endeavour to observe a few seconds' pause before you reply.

b) Even better, if your partner is willing, mentally repeat the point they made before you formulate your response.

c) Better still, try putting yourself in their place and see how they have come to hold that belief or opinion.

### Healing Practice: Accommodation rather than Compromise

We have all had the experience of feeling stuck and driven to prevarication when we can't make a choice between two unpalatable alternatives. This is usually expressed something along the lines of: "I don't want to do xxxxx, but if I don't do that I'll have to do xxx! But I don't want to do either!" This is an example of 'either/or' dualistic thinking. Our society habitually calls for a compromise which is defined as 'settling a dispute by making concessions on both sides'. I have never yet met anyone who is happy with a compromise or have been able to give their energy wholeheartedly to this halfway solution.

If you find yourself in this situation then search for an accommodation: 'adjust, adapt, bring to an agreement'. This is a solution arrived at by lateral thinking. It usually takes the consideration of a range of alternatives to come to a third and 'higher' position to which you (and another) can commit yourselves.

Consider and enact some *'both/and'* alternatives rather than 'either/or' and see how that can change your life.

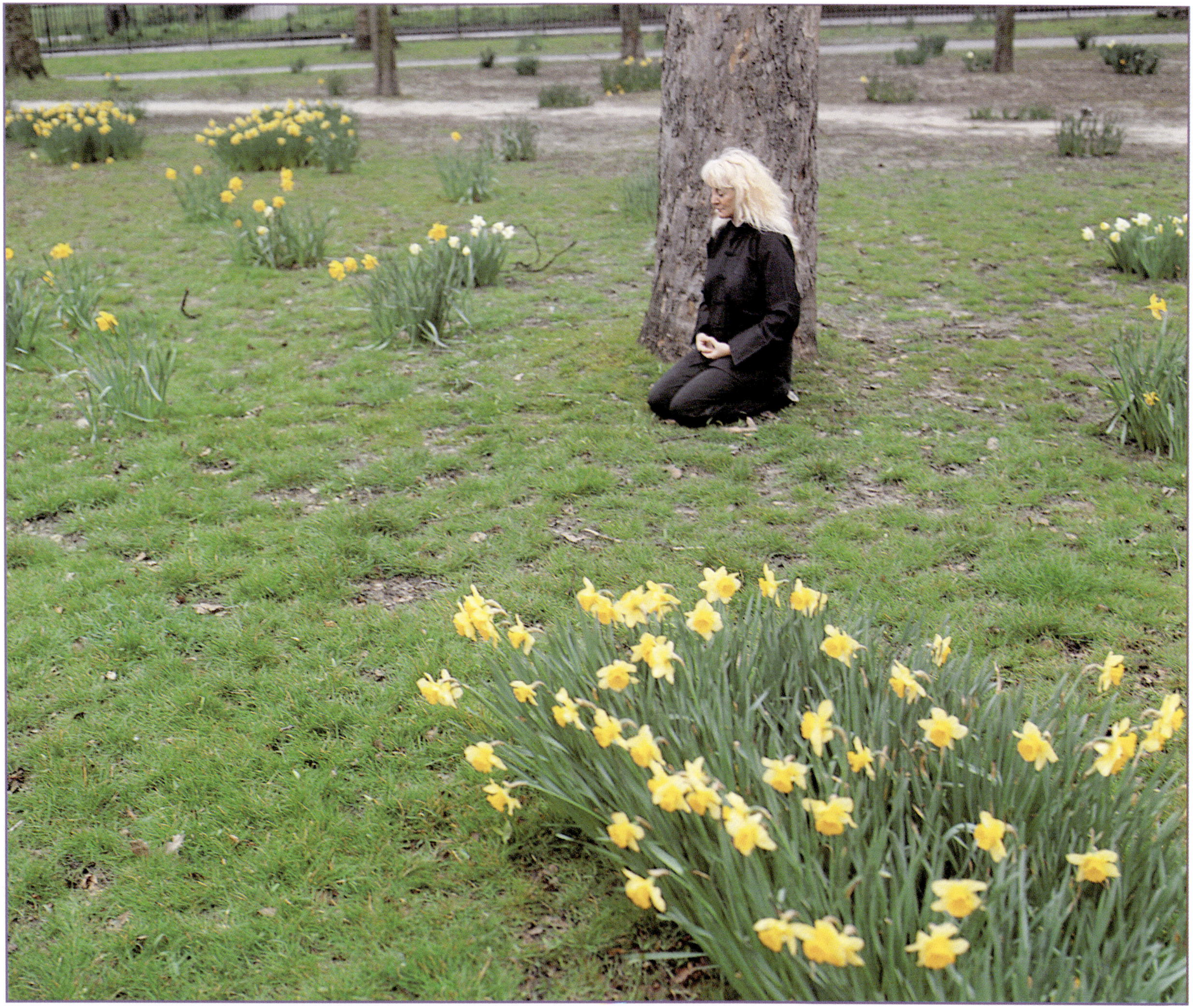

# HEALING YOUR RELATIONSHIPS

*"Love possesses not, nor would it be possessed."*

### Relationships With Partners

So often we choose a partner on the basis of need, and this can be on a number of levels: you require physical/material skills (money-making, practical, etc.), there is an emotional lack in yourself (you need someone who has qualities you believe you don't possess; calmness, empathy etc.), mental skills (stimulation, learning, teaching etc.). So often, particularly in Western culture, the relationship is based on the fact that the other person is the catalyst or trigger that puts you into that wonderful space of being in love!

As that rascally sage, Ram Dass (Dr. Richard Alpert), points out: "We all start out deprived or starved of love, so we close down and are caught inside ourselves. Then, one day, we meet somebody who has the key that opens something within us and we say 'I'm in love, wow!' And when you're in love everything's beautiful and sweet and soft. And we say: 'I'm in love with you!' A truer way of expressing it would be: 'You are my connection that opens me to the place in myself where I am in love.'" Unfortunately we get very attached to our connection because we don't know how to bring ourselves to the place within us where we are in love.

When two people are each other's connection, each has the key stimulus that releases the mechanism that opens them to their hearts, they say: "We are in love with each other, let's be together, let's nest!" Unfortunately, the 'thing' that was your connection (for instance passion) can be subject to change. If you are 'imprinted', then this love response is likely to release itself under similar conditions with another person, with all the hurt, heartache and social upheaval that that entails.

We are all working on a 'deprivation schedule', where we've been so out of love. We feel we want to collect all the connections so we won't run out. You don't have to – there's no end to them, they won't run out. Love is not something you need a someone to release. The only long-term solution is to find that space of awareness that's within you all the time, and rest in it.

### Heartache & Heartbreak

It used to be considered a 'truism' that opposites attract. Recent studies and psychological experiment actually shows a tendency to bond with partners on the basis of similarity. In fact, we are most likely to choose a heterosexual mate who we elect to be our male or female complement. In the case of animal/pet owners, this gets sublimated to such an extent that pets often look like their owners either physically or temperamentally!

Heartache or heartbreak results when our partners refuse to accept the role we impose, often because of the implied responsibility that entails. How healthy can it be to look for these attributes in someone else rather than within ourselves? Eventually, our partner will crack under the strain. Just as, energetically, in the whole and compassionate heart the two complementary energies of male and female, red and white, salt and mercury, Shiva and Shakti, combine and merge, we unconsciously seek this union in the outer form, i.e. with another human being.

If you have ever had your heart 'broken', there is a natural tendency to say 'they broke my heart' instead of the truer 'I broke my heart over them'. So many popular songs deal with the subject of heartbreak. We've all heard the version that goes: "My heart's been broken. I'm gonna build a fortress round my heart so I won't get hurt again." The problem is it gets lonely behind the ramparts after a while. A hardened heart that is not reaching out with sympathy to engage in feeling becomes cold and under-nourished. Alright, sometimes we need a coping mechanism when life becomes unbearable but ultimately we have to 'deal' with a situation ourselves. In the long term we have to learn to strike a balance between keeping our heart open and sensitive to pain and suffering, yet balanced with the knowledge that everything is lawful and unfolding in a perfectly natural way.

### Relationships with Children

The way in which we relate to our children varies according to where we are in the cycle of our lives. This passage encapsulates the sometimes difficult relationship:

"Your children are not your children. They are the sons and daughters of life's longing for itself. They come through you but not from you, and though they are with you yet they belong not to you . . . You are the bows from which your children as living arrows are sent forth."

'The Prophet' – Kahil Gibrain

### Relationships With Parents

Getting to grips with relationships with one's parents goes straight to the heart of so many energetic confusions. Our earthly parents reflect our attitudes towards the divine archetypes of mother and father.

So many people harbour grief, anger, hatred towards dead parents and often bitterly regret not being reconciled to them, "and now it's too late". It's never too late, you can be reconciled to them at any time, living or dead. You don't even have to see them!

Too often, in their grief, people seek the help, comfort or intermediary help of the psychic/clairvoyant. Although helpful in some regards, nevertheless, this approach is to mistake the outer form for the inner. The real healing work must be completed internally.

### Healing Practice:
### Take A Seat

1. Set two chairs facing each other and sit in one of them.

2. Invite your father or mother to sit before you. Spend a minute or two imagining their form, mannerisms, smile, clothing, etc. Do not be alarmed if you feel a real sense of their presence. Do not be afraid, you are inviting them into a space of peace and good humour.

3. Firstly, acknowledge the primary emotion you feel towards them. Voice it, e.g. "You make me so angry . . .etc". This is your chance to tell them how you feel, to express anger, sadness, loss, loving concern. For some of you this may be the first time you honestly express your feelings. Please do not be disturbed if this flow of thoughts becomes a torrent – the longer things have been repressed and the deeper they have been buried, the more energetic and powerful the release.

4. Once you have 'discharged', spoken your

and compassion for your own suffering.

7. Before your parent leaves your presence, forgive them their actions and human failings, forgive yourself for your reactions and 'negative' expressions of emotion. Bless them, bless yourself and release all the energies generated into the air to be scattered harmlessly into the wind.

**Take A Letter**
Another useful way of expressing your thoughts and feelings is by letter. Whether living or dead, compose a letter to each of your parents.

**Option 1:** Before you write, determine that you will not send it. Your thoughts could then be as honest as you wish. When you feel you have, for instance, 'asked forgiveness' or expressed the 'forbidden' questions, then burn or destroy the letter as you send it on its way with love and a blessing.

**Option 2:** Write a series of letters composed periodically. Keep them as a record of your developing thoughts. Once you have done this a few times you will find that the contents of your letters change, become either more focused or clearer and more lucid. We have all seen movies where adult offspring find a bundle of love letters or diaries, belonging to their parents, in the attic. Often, understanding they are human beings like ourselves, with the same drives, fears, etc., can be a real eye-opener.

**Option 3:** Regularly continue your processing until you feel clear and more sure of yourself. You might even be ready to send a heartfelt letter.

**Co-Listening**
*"Let the voice within your voice speak to the ear of his voice."*
No one really teaches us how to listen and, because of that, we are always at risk of a breakdown in communication with our partners, friends, siblings, parents and colleagues. What I would like to see is more of these lifestyle skills taught to children in school. It is far more valuable than so many of the archaic, academic programmes and I feel sure that children, especially

truth or asked the question(s) you always wanted to ask, sit quietly and wait for a response. Sometimes your parent will speak to your mind and answer/reflect your question or emotion. Sit quietly, pause for a minute and make your response (if necessary).

5. The other option is to change seats and pretend to be your parent. Now imagine yourself sitting opposite. Conjure your form and see the emotions written on your face or in your posture. How would your parent respond to you?

6. Continue the dialogue until you are satisfied that there has been an energy exchange, both ways. Repeat this practice for both parents and as often as you wish. In time you may come to understand who they are and why they acted/reacted as they did towards you. The aim is to get to the stage where you have compassion for their attitudes and actions

those with learning difficulties, would benefit greatly from this easy healing practice. Co-listening (in its many forms) is a valued source of learning how to listen not just to other people but to ourselves. So often our inner voice is speaking to us and we ignore it, only to regret it later. Here is a sample of how to co-listen with someone. It can be a great way of healing difficult relationships and deepening others.

### Healing Practice

1. Sit facing your partner, holding hands if you so wish.

2. One of you start off by talking uninterrupted for up to three minutes. If you are the listener do not to be tempted to nod or respond in any way. Allow for silent periods as these are so often the times when your partner is struggling to voice the point they need to make.

3. The conversation can be about anything but preferably the first thing that comes to mind.

4. Whoever was the listener replies by repeating, as accurately as possible, what the speaker had been saying.

5. Repeat the practice with reversed roles. Finally, feel free to each comment on what the other person has said without any judgement or well-meant solution to a problem that may have come up. Observe your conversation and try not to compromise but rather accommodate each other's needs where necessary. There never seems to be a solution when compromise is considered.

6. Remember to thank your partner for the time and energy/space they have given you and finish by making a positive observation about them personally (even if it is only to comment on their style of dress!)

# HEALING YOUR EMOTIONS

*"Bless you for your anger for it is a sign of rising energy. Direct not to your family, waste not on your enemy. Transform the energy to versatility and it will bring you prosperity."*

Rainbow Revelation – Yoko Ono

First and foremost, it is healthy to allow your emotions to surface. Suppressed anger, fear, hatred, jealousy, sorrow, greed, self-doubt and, of course, love, can cause despair, depression and ultimately disease.

When your emotions bubble to the surface they can, in fact, be a blessing in disguise. Each one offers you the chance to redirect misguided energy. They could be likened to a growing plant with tangled roots and no source of nourishment. Every emotion could be a different flower with special qualities. Here is a way of allowing your own flowers to blossom in the garden of life.

### Anger
When anger rises, be flexible in the way you view it. Observe it burning out of you, expressing it physically like stamping through the park or digging up the garden.

### Fear
Forgive yourself for being fearful. Give yourself some tender loving care. Your inner self is crying out for reassurance.

### Greed
Balance your giving with your taking. Life is about asking, giving and taking. If this is not fully realized, there will be a build-up of frustration that can engender a grasping, greedy attitude as a result of imbalanced energies within.

### Jealousy
Learning to admire other people's qualities, including your own, adds validity to these qualities. Being interested in other people can boost your own confidence by reducing self-consciousness and doubt.

### Lack of Love
Open your heart to love. The absence of love in your life can be caused by suppressing your natural feelings and not allowing yourself to love and be loved.

30

# HEALING YOUR BODY

*"Movement is Life."*

One of the key aims of this book is to help highlight the areas of your life that need help and attention. They could take the form of helping to evaluate your use of energy or helping you to cope with an acute illness. Better still, try to find the root cause of your suffering and set up a healthful plan of action, one that is realistic, yet at the same time enjoyable .

It is easy to see why movement in one form or another, be it dance, sport or exercise is wholeheartedly recommended by professionals in virtually every field of health care.

Your body exists, not just to be maintained but for your own use and enjoyment. Beyond that, your body contains just about every tool it needs to heal itself. Movement is one of the most versatile and enjoyable of these tools.

The best response to using movement in a balanced way is by being aware of your posture and how you use it in everyday movements.

### Healing Practices

- Posture. The Alexander Technique specializes in corrective posture work. Just 'growing' up through the spine and thinking of your head as a flower on a flexible stem, feet rooted into the earth, is a good starting point.

- Yoga helps to alleviate and prevent many ailments with its remedial exercises.

- Pace Yourself. Relaxation and meditation are excellent ways of learning how to pace yourself.

- Tai Chi, Qi Gong, Yogarhythm helps you to flow with the rhythms of life and to balance your bodily, mental and spiritual energies.

- Awareness and a changed attitude can enhance the overall condition of your body from being rigid and inflexible to mobile and fluid – tense to relaxed – abused to fully used – numb to fully alive and alert.

- 'Beating yourself up' is something you can do without always realizing and is always counter-productive. We, in the West, are particularly cruel to ourselves in ways which many in the Orient find difficult to understand. Much of this angry energy is born out of frustration and an inability to balance the male and female principles. Beating up cushions or a punchbag is one of the best ways to physically get rid of these emotions. The answer is not to fight yourself, but to acknowledge your anger and dissipate it by allowing the energy to flow away in order to feel the depths of your own loving kindness and compassion. Act from the heart and let your religion be kindness.

# HEALING THROUGH YOUR SENSES

*"Your body is the Harp of your Soul and it is yours to bring forth sweet music from its confused sounds."*

The theme of the senses, in case you hadn't noticed, has been weaving its way throughout the whole of this book. You need your senses to provide warning signals of any health problems you may have. The mind is the main receptor of the information picked up by the senses. The great thing about using them as a healing tool is that you can enjoy the process of getting better so much more.

Your commonsense approach will give you an open-ended way to full self-development. The knowledge of how to help yourself through your senses will emerge from your own experiences. Learning to trust your senses and responding by taking responsibility does work and cannot be underestimated. You can be fully involved in your own transformation by tuning in and seeking guidance to help bring thoughts into being.

## SOUND
*"In the beginning was the Word..."*

Listening to the 'sound of silence' can be one of the most beneficial practices for, unless you are profoundly deaf, there is no such thing as absolute silence. The reason why so many of us suffer from stressful conditions is that we are constantly assailed by repetitive sound and are suffering as a result. Our towns and cities are becoming noisier and the natural sounds of the countryside are becoming a mere echo of the past for city dwellers.

Your ears collect sounds from the outside world, the outer point of your ear or pinna, picking up and directing sounds into the ear. You can increase the amount of sound collected by cupping your hand behind the ear. The canal directs the sounds into your eardrum. In the canal are tiny hairs and waxy fluid which traps dirt and keeps the canal clean. The sounds start the eardrum vibrating which are then picked up and interpreted by the brain.

We can enhance the effects of sound by singing, chanting, talking, humming, sighing. Meditation is a way of learning how to become part of silence, and the sounds you are hearing.

For some, laughter is the melody of the soul but music could equally be given that special accolade. Nature provides a daily orchestra of sounds, so the mere fact of sitting outside can have a effect on us for the better. There are certain subliminal sounds, even natural ones, that we put up with or don't even hear. These can come to include the voices of our spouse or children until we cease to listen to them any more. I had a friend with a whining, monotonous voice who, no matter how she tried, never seemed to have lasting meaningful relationships, until she altered the tone of her voice and the depth of her breathing.

Sound must be approached with a spirit of awareness. If you are going to heal your life through sound it may be that the fundamental step you need to take is to listen to sounds in general, then to your own sounds and then to learn the art of listening. The Chinese believe we need to listen with our hearts and say thank you afterwards for having the gift of being able to do so at all.

Health problems can actually be cured by sound waves. There are hemi-synch tapes which produce different sounds in different hemispheres of the brain that are actually balancing the male/female, left/right sides of the brain on the physical level, which helps with meditation, deep relaxation and sleeping. There are special Indian ragas that are played at certain times of the day with yantras (visual representations of the sounds themselves) and mandalas (visual designs reflecting divine properties). People are healed with these practices. Colour also plays an integral part as different colours are used for different ragas.

The sound of kindness in someone's voice can effect us deeply. So it is not just what you say, but the way that you say it. If there is an echo of truth (resonance) then the effects are lasting. On a practical front it could probably be more appropriate for us to have a holiday from sound, not having to respond with sounds or words can be most relaxing.

In the Chinese tradition, sound can express disharmony or harmony from within the body, e.g. laughter is the heart meridian but too much can cause heart failure. People have actually died laughing although I can't think of a better way to go. The liver has a kind of groaning sound, lungs a brief sighing. Just going into a room and expressing whatever sound you feel like can be most helpful/healthful.

Playing a musical instrument is another way of expressing emotion through sound. Just talking with yourself and other people can impart a sense of balance.

### Taking Care of Your Ears & Hearing
The most common kind of infection occurs in the middle ear. Germs can easily travel up the eustacian tube to the ear, especially when you have a cold. Blowing your nose too hard can force the cold germs up the tube. It is always advisable to go to the doctor with any ear infections.

Hardened earwax can cause deafness and discomfort. Avoid using your fingers or cotton buds. A little warm olive oil gently inserted into the ear canal will soften the wax and help it to easily disperse.

### Healing Practice
Bhramari or Humming Bee Breath, is a yogic practice which instills confidence and a sense of deep inner peace.

1. Sit upright in a comfortable, yet well-appointed chair, feet on the ground, knees in line with hips, hands resting on the thighs, crown of the head in line with the base vertebrae, spine leaning slightly forwards to allow for easy breathing movements in the lower part of the lungs.

2. Exhale to release any stale air.

3. Inhale slowly and fully. Contract your base muscles (anus, uterus, lower abdominal muscles).

4. Raise the chest slightly, locking the chin down without clenching your teeth.

5. Straighten the arms and raise the shoulders by pressing the hands against your thighs or knees to strengthen the chin lock.

6. Hold your breath for as long as is reasonably comfortable.

7. Release the base lock, relax your shoulders, raise your head to release the chin lock.

8. Block your ears by gently pressing stopping your ears with the middle fingers.

9. Exhale slowly and evenly with a humming bee sound until all the air has been released.

10. Repeat the sequence for up to 10 or 15 minutes. If you wish, or your breathing requires it, sit quietly whilst taking 2 or 3 natural breaths between each repetition.

## SIGHT

*"There is a healing light shining in the Centre of my Being."*

The element of sight that is most often discussed is not so much form and texture as colour. It works on at least three different levels. On the physical level we now know that even the foetus in the womb perceives the colour red through the amniotic fluid. It is less well known that there are colour receptors in the skin. There is a body of evidence that suggests that it is possible to identify colour through the fingertips.

On an emotional level, we are all used to describing moods and feelings by associating them with colours: "I just saw red", "I took a jaundiced (yellow) view", "I was green with envy", "I had the blues", "I was in a black mood", etc.

The problem is that various cultures ascribe different values to the same colour. In Western tradition, for instance, white is a symbol of purity, while in the Orient it signifies death. This has led to a range of misunderstandings when using colour as a therapy tool. One of the classic misconceptions of the 1940s and '50s was the use of a medium green-coloured paint in the decoration of hospitals and mental institutions. It was a drastic mistake. For patients with low energy or depression, this unstimulating colour had the effect of worsening their condition. Conversely, if you were to put a heart patient with an excitable metabolic rate in a red room, they would most likely be overstimulated to a detrimental degree. Any use of colour therapy would therefore need to be tailored to the individual.

On a mental/psychological level, it is a question of attitude. There is a Buddhist saying: *"The biggest obstacle to seeing is the eye."* It may be through the physical sense of sight that we perceive objects or people but it is through the mind that we form judgements on what we see, although it is said that: *"To someone who is pure, all things appear pure"*. This leads us to the question of intention. The Native Americans have a saying: *"If you leave your dwelling place with the intention of looking for the enemy, you'll find them."* Finally, belief. It is an unfortunate truism that *"We see what we believe rather than believe what we see."*

• **Kindly Looks:** To look upon someone kindly can generate a healing power of its own. This aptitude cannot be plucked from the air but can be cultivated with practice. Pick someone for whom, at this time, you feel little sympathy. Use the practice of Tong-Len to transform your view so that you come to regard them with kindness and equanimity. When you can accomplish this you will find that you can suspend judgement, improving your relationships as a result.

• **Fixed Attention Meditation:** This ancient technique, practised in almost every culture, is recognized as a powerful way to improve concentration. Fix your gaze on an object at about an arm's length and at eye level. Any object will do, although a meditator might use a candle flame in more advanced practice. Unwavering, unblinking, wide-eyed attention will bring about 'tearing' which in itself is a therapeutic method of expelling grit and dirt as well as toxins and waste products.

• Rub your hands together vigorously for a minute or two, then gently place them over your closed eyelids for a soothing, restorative effect.

## TOUCH
*"Touch teaches the healer."*

It is hard to imagine what it would be like not to be able to touch and feel. This sense gives so much pleasure as well as relief. If, however, you are in pain then you might think otherwise. Pain protects us from harm: it is nature's way of issuing warning signals that we should stop what we are doing and take care of ourselves. Where emotional pain is concerned, there is a chance that, if it has already existed a long time and become deeply embedded, we can become inured to it.

### Healing Practices

- Cuddling, hugging and kissing are a great source of comfort, especially where words are inappropriate.

- Stroking and caring for our animals has been proven to be beneficial to the heart and helps regulate blood pressure.

- Love-making is a wonderful 'universal' cure and preventative for many complaints such as headaches and migraines.

- Massage is rapidly growing in popularity and has endless potential, especially for the elderly who long for a loving touch in their lives.

- Aqua-therapy, such as swimming (especially in the sea), showering and bathing are ways in which you can imagine that you are washing away disease and worry.

- Self-healing. Start by closing your eyes and picturing in your mind's eye your pain or discomfort . . . place one or both of your hands on or above the area and imagine that it has a colour . . . shape . . . size . . . texture. . . smell. Now give it an 'escape route', e.g. down or up the spine . . . arms . . . legs . . . crown . . . head . . . orifices. With each consecutive breath, imagine the pain moving along the channels of escape, e.g. through railway lines along the spine and out through the crown. Now picture your pain outside the body. See any changes that have occurred. Repeat the process, noting any changes. If you have difficulty releasing the pain, then encourage it by gently squeezing with your supportive 'mother' hand. Once you feel and see that the pain has come out, gently imagine placing your other hand over it and pressing it down into the soft 'welcoming' earth. Imagine nature absorbing and dispersing your pain.

## SMELL & TASTE

*"If you bake bread with indifference, you bake a bitter bread."*

Smell and taste are interrelated. You sometimes actually seem to 'taste' a smell, and vice versa. Your sense of smell helps you recognize the danger of escaping gas, rotting food, fire. The problem is that you only notice new smells for a short time because your 'smell receptors' quickly become accustomed to them. Conversely, there are certain smells that have a therapeutic effect such as freshly baked bread or sea breezes.

### Healing Practices

- Eat your way to good health. One sure way of maintaining a sound constitution is to adopt a nutritionally sound pattern of eating. Food is transformed into physical energy so it is important to select the right kind to supply your body with the elements required for its complete harmonious function. This will enable you to utilize your potential energy to its best possible advantage. Your body is not a mere machine, but a living, vital organism and because of this you need to take care what you put into it.

Combining your foods is an important step in the fundamental reforms needed to maintain a well-balanced body weight. If you are perfectly healthy and lead a vigorous outdoor life, then combining foods such as starch and protein will have no harmful after-effects; but if you have a fairly sedentary life, or a stressful one, with mental, physical and emotional tensions, then starches and proteins need to be kept apart as much as possible.

# Ideal Food Combinations

1. *Starches & Fats*:
   Bread and butter, cereals & cream, bananas & cream.

2. *Starches & Green Vegetables:*
   Bread or other cereals and green vegetables, potatoes and greens, cucumber, lettuce or watercress sandwiches.

3. *Starches, Fats & Green Vegetables:*
   Bread & butter, green salad & olive oil dressing, bananas & cream.

4. *Starches & Sugars:* Bread & honey, cereals & honey.

5. *Starches & Dried Fruits:* Cereals & dates, raisins, figs.

6. *Starches, Sugars & Dried Fruits:*
   Green salad with raisins and olive oil dressing, bread & butter.

7. *Starches, Fats, Dried Fruits, Green Vegetables:*
   Green salad with sultanas or dried apricots, olive oil, bread & butter.

8. *Protein & Acid Fruits:*
   Milk and fresh fruits, cheese and fresh fruits, meat and fresh fruits.

9. *Protein & Green Vegetables:* Meat, fish or eggs with steamed vegetables, i.e. spinach, or green salad.

10. *Protein & Fats:* Fish and butter sauce, fat meats, i.e. bacon, are examples of proteins and fats that combine naturally.

11. *Proteins, Fats & Green Vegetables:*
    Roast beef and green vegetables, poached egg on spinach with butter.

12. *Proteins, Fats & Acid Fruits:*
    Roast pork with apple sauce, grilled fish or meat with butter and a sprinkling of lemon juice, nuts and apples.

13. *Fats & Acid Fruits:*
    Fresh fruit & cream.

14. *Fats & Sugars:*
    Dried fruit & nuts, dried fruit & cream, stewed fruit and cream.

15. *Sugars & Protein:*
    Honey & milk, dried fruit & milk.

## Unwise Combinations
### (for sedentary lifestyles)
1. Proteins & Starches
2. Starches & Acid Fruits

37

# HERBAL & FLOWER FIRST AID

These natural remedies are quite safe, provided they are treated with respect. Keeping a herbal first-aid kit in your home or for travel purposes can be most valuable. The greatest problem with self-treatment lies in not obtaining professional advice when it is indicated. So please use your common sense.
**Note:** If you are taking long-term medication prescribed by your G.P. or hospital, it is advisable to check with a medical herbalist.

**Bach Flower Remedies**
These special remedies are now used worldwide. They are named after an Englishman called Dr. Edward Bach who invented them after a severe illness of his own. Bach found he was able to intuitively judge the healing properties of different plants and spent many years experimenting and making up his own remedies.

His methods of production are still used today and are designed to treat the whole person rather than just the symptoms of the disease. The principle behind their use is the fact that every disorder, physical or psychological, arises because of an inner imbalance for which nature has provided a cure in the form of healing plants, sunlight, spring water and fresh air. They are chosen according to physiological and emotional symptoms but are still able to help physical ailments and are perfectly safe provided that orthodox treatment is taken, where necessary.

## A Guide To Use

1. When choosing a Bach Flower Remedy, try to examine, as honestly as possible, your mental and emotional state, habits, attitudes, behavioural patterns.

2. Use no more than five at any one time, generally the fewer the better.

3. Some remedies may need to be taken for longer than others, depending on your nature and personality.

4. Select the remedies that appeal to you and experiment with them.

5. All instructions for use are clearly given with the remedies when you purchase them.

6. Take a few drops of the dilute remedy four times a day, including first thing in the morning and last thing at night. The drops can either be taken in a little spring water or dropped straight onto the tongue (ensure your tongue does not touch the dropper for hygienic reasons).

7. When you take the remedy, imagine it as a healing light penetrating your whole being.

8. It is quite safe for children and animals to take the remedies, but please check instructions carefully as to the quantities needed.

9. Keep dilute remedies in a fridge in hot weather or else in a cool dark place after use.

10. Check before using each remedy that it is still fresh.

Bach Flower Remedies can be purchased from most health food shops or directly from:
Bach Centre, Unit 6, Suffolk Way, Abingdon, Oxon OX14 5JX, U.K.

## Choosing Your Remedy

**Agrimony:** Hiding your worries behind a cheerful face.
**Aspen:** Apprehensive for unknown reason.
**Beech:** Critical and intolerant of others.
**Centaury:** Weak willed, easily exploited
or imposed upon.
**Cerato:** Doubting your own judgement.
**Cherry Plum:** Fear, tension, irrational thinking.
**Chestnut Bud:** Refusing to learn by experience and repeating the same mistakes.
**Chicory:** Self-centred, possessive, clinging, overprotective towards loved ones.
**Clematis:** Inattentive, dreamy, absent-minded, escapist.
**Crab Apple:** Cleanser for self-disgust, prudishness, over-consciousness of personal ailments.
**Elm:** Feeling of inadequacy, overwhelming responsibility.
**Gentian:** Despondency.
**Gorse:** Feelings of hopelessness, pessimism, defeatism.
**Heather:** Overtalkative, obsessive over personal problems and experiences.
**Holly:** Hatred, envy, jealousy, suspicion.
**Honeysuckle:** Living in the past, homesickness.
**Hornbeam:** Mental fatigue, procrastination.
**Impatiens:** Irritability, impatience.
**Larch:** Lack of self-confidence, inferiority complex, fear of failure.
**Mimulus:** Black moods for no apparent reason.
**Oak:** No longer able to struggle bravely against illness or adversity even though you have a natural, courageous spirit.
**Olive:** Exhaustion caused by long-standing problems.
**Pine:** Guilt, blaming yourself for other people's mistakes.
**Red Chestnut:** Obsessive care and concern for others.
**Rock Rose:** Panic and fear.
**Rock Water:** Inflexible mind, self-denial.
**Scleranthus:** Fluctuating moods, indecisive.

| | |
|---|---|
| Star of Bethlehem: | Shock and grief. |
| Sweet Chestnut: | Despair and negative outlook. |
| Vervain: | Over-enthusiastic, fanatical beliefs. |
| Vine: | Autocratic, arrogant, domineering, inflexible. |
| Walnut: | Puberty, menopause, divorce, changes in home or work environment. |
| Water Violet: | Proud, reserved, aloof, self-contained. |
| White Chestnut: | Preoccupation with worry, mental conflict, persistent unwanted thoughts. |
| Wild Oat: | Lack of clarity over your direction in life. |
| Wild Rose: | Apathy, resignation. |
| Willow: | Embittered, resentful. |

### Rescue Remedy

This is a combination of cherry plum, clematis, impatiens, rock rose and star of Bethlehem. It is an all-purpose treatment used for any kind of shock, illness, injury or trauma and is said to help restore calmness after an accident or painful experience. Also available in cream form for use on cuts, grazes, burns and bites as well as skin conditions such as eczema. Note: It is not recommended for long-term use and does not replace medical treatment.

# HEALING YOUR ENVIRONMENT

*"Weave the path of life and living throughout eternity and see the expansiveness of the eternal plan."*

All too often we put our energies into re-evaluating our general environment and striving to change it, whereas the real answer lie in re-evaluating our own bodies. This is more likely to be where the most valuable transformations are needed. This is not to say that we should not be conscious of our environment, especially the wider world in which we live, far from it. In so far as we can control it, it is a reflection of our general philosophy of life.

Taking care of your immediate environment is an excellent starting point. You could pause and take stock to see if your domestic surroundings reflect the part of your life that needs a change for the better.

It is unnecessary to spend a fortune on your home in order to create an atmosphere of peace and harmony. Simply painting walls another colour, putting a few flowers in a vase or decorating with natural objects such as shells, stones and candles can produce a subtle quality which will bring pleasure to the senses. Airing your home and disposing of objects and clothes that you no longer need liberates you by providing more space that will be easier to maintain and keep clean. Giving your body a good spring clean both inside and out can have much the same effect. Fasting is a way of 'spring-cleaning' but it needs to be carefully monitored. A one-day fast of fruit juices or brown rice is a practice guaranteed to give your digestive system a good rest and allow you to get rid of unwanted toxins.

# EXPLORING YOUR SUBTLE HEALING ENERGIES

This is a practice that can be done after any of the previous techniques, once a state of stabilization has occurred. An added practice for releasing emotions is massaging the acupressure point on the palm of the hand. This is a refinement of a natural movement we sometimes make; when we're overwrought, we often wring our hands. This has the effect of energizing the palms of our hands, our most obvious healing tool. Another way of concentrating energy to the hands is to rub them briskly together.

**Healing Practice**

- This practice can be performed either standing (as in the traditional Tai Chi way), or sitting on a chair. Close your eyes to avoid distraction.

- Bring the palms of your hands together and generate heat by rubbing them together briskly.

- Hold them comfortably in front of your body to explore the 'sphere/ball' of space between your hands.

- You may feel a tingling sensation, magnetism, elasticity, change of temperature. Be aware of the interplay of emotions with the moving form of your sphere.

- Now extend that feeling to explore the outside of your body by running the hands over the 'etheric' layer or 'aura' without touching the body. Be sensitive to any changes.

- If you are drawn to any particular area, concentrate on the energy to find out more about it.

- Disease sometimes shows up as excessive heat or cold, depending on the type of disease or dysfunction.

- Concentrate your mind on these areas to try to stimulate the natural capacity to bring imbalances into harmony and to encourage the healing process to occur.

- Allow your body to inform you of its needs in the same way a baby communicates its needs to its mother. When you feel confident, try practising on your family and friends.

# HEALING YOUR LIFE

**Tong-Len, Root Practice for Eradicating Suffering**

The following procedures are required for any of the mind practices such as visualization, concentration or relaxation.

**Preparation of the Room**

This is a helpful procedure for all types of healing and meditational practices.

Prepare a room or space that is quiet, at a comfortable temperature, free from interruptions (put on answerphone), where you can find a balance between being relaxed and alert.

**Preparation of the Body**
Let common sense prevail. Things to avoid:
- A noisy environment
- A heavy meal before practice which can produce drowsiness.
- Conversely, lack of food can also lead to poor concentration.
- A busy schedule when you have to rush off somewhere immediately afterwards.
- Practising when exhausted.
- Drugs or alcohol.
- Restrictive clothing.
- A full bladder.

These following body preparations are helpful for discovering and correcting mis-alignments in posture.

**Sitting Positions and Postures**
- Sit on a postural chair (if you have back problems) or a meditation stool or cross-legged. Use a firm cushion to raise hips higher than the knees if you are sitting on the ground.
- Lean the spine slightly forward to allow for ease of breathing in lower lungs.
- Rest hands on the knees in any way which feels comfortable.
- If seated on a chair, raise the hips on a cushion, if required.
- Have knees in line with the centre of the feet, shoulder-width apart.
- Rest hands on the thighs.
- Relax shoulders but avoid hunching or a rigid 'military set'.
- The spine should be unsupported if possible and fractionally forward.

**Sitting on a Chair**

The feet should be a hip- or shoulder-width apart, parallel, the knees in line with the centre of the foot, the hips raised, possibly with the help of an extra cushion (if required). This enables a free flow of energy throughout the body. Hands should be placed palm down on the knees, relaxing the shoulders and avoiding slumping or hunching or a rigid 'military set'. The tip of the tongue should rest naturally on the upper palate on the line between the teeth and the gums. In many spiritual traditions this links the circuit of energy flowing throughout the body. It has the added advantage of slowing down the saliva output. Continual swallowing during deep or intensive practice would be a distraction. As a final compassionate touch, permit yourself a subtle inner smile.

The following practice is useful as a daily meditation. As you become more adept you should be able to practise anytime, anywhere. From here on, there are different meditations you can do from this posture.

**Visualization**

Concentrate on the top of the head, imagine a silken thread pulling/stretching the whole body upwards as though the skull were being suspended by a silken thread. Visualize the vertebrae as beads on a silken cord/thread. Experience the fluidity of movement from such a viewpoint. On the in-breath, extend the spine upwards and on the out-breath gently relax the muscles around the body structure. Resist the tendency to sink into the hips and slump the body. On the last out-breath, gently lean the body fractionally forward and feel the energetic difference. Don't be concerned if the difference is not immediately apparent, this will come with practice.

**Checking the Body Tension**

Concentrate your attention on the top of the scalp. On the in-breath, slightly tense, on the out-breath, gently release the tension and allow a sensation or visualize the energy draining downwards through your body. Gently work your way through the body, i.e. relax facial tension, neck, shoulders, stomach or any areas of tension stored in the body.

At the end of the practice, imagine the tension draining into the ground and discharging. The exercise can be intensified by the association of emotions connected in various areas of the body. (To re-energize your body, breathe in, bringing the energy upwards and through the top of the head, discharging any tension. Reverse the procedure and breathe in energy through the top of the body and down through the body. The practice is limited only by your imagination and the time you allow.

By now, your body should be in a comfortable position, relaxed and ready to approach the mind practices.

**Stabilizing of the Breath**

Stabilize body and mind energies through concentration on the breath. Without altering the breath, but simply observing it, concentrate the mind on the area below the nostrils and on the upper lip. Simply watch and feel the flow of the breath in and out of the body.

Let the mind relax in this awareness. If thoughts arise, recognize them and let them go. If it is a 'good' or pleasant thought, be aware of the tendency to try and keep it. Recognize this habit and relax and let go. If a 'bad' thought arises be aware of the tendency to push it away or deny it. Recognize this habit, accept the thought and simultaneously let it go. Return the mind to concentrating on the point of attention already selected. If the attention wanders, recognize it and without blame or judgement, gently bring the mind home. Whether the thoughts appear to be

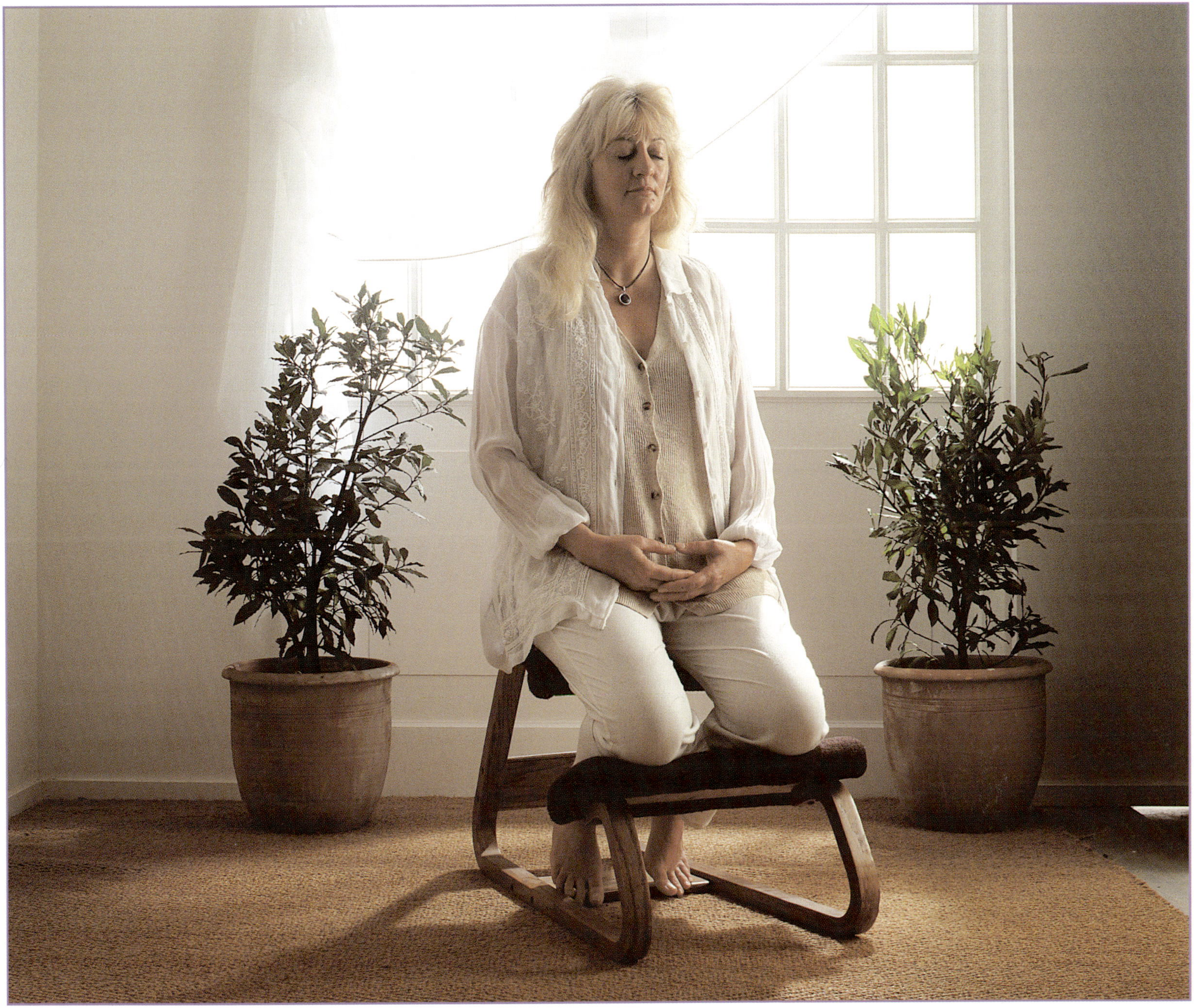

faster or slower, accept each one for what it is, another thought, and let that dissolve also.

A common misunderstanding in meditation is that we must empty the mind. This is an impossible task, for thoughts come unbidden. If you tried to remove 'bad' reflections from a mirror or keep only the 'good' reflections you would soon realize that this is similarly impossible. The nature of the mirror is to reflect everything, without any process of discrimination. Similarly, the mind should be relaxed so that we can be at peace within our thoughts.

Another way of viewing this process is that we wish to find our lost peace of mind. Imagine the mind as a pool of water in which we have lost something. If we take a stick and attempt to find what we are looking for by poking about on the bottom of the pool, all we succeed in doing is stirring up the mud and clouding the water. If we cease to disturb the water, the mud will gradually settle, the water will clarify naturally and we will be able to see clearly again. Any thought could be visualized as a stone dropping into the pool. We could watch the ripples extend from the epicentre and gradually disappear until gradually the water becomes as still as a mill pool reflecting an empty sky.

If we are searching for the nature of our true mind it may be helpful to regard it as our inner 'sun'. It radiates its warmth in all directions. If our thoughts are cloudy they may temporarily obscure the sun so that we forget the endless continuation of that radiance. If we attach too much importance to the clouds we may forget that the sun is always there. Our own radiant nature is always there, we simply have to let go of all that is in the way of our understanding this.

The practice of meditation on the breath is the practice of one-pointedness or concentration. The benefits are many, including relaxation of tension of the body and the mind, increased ability to concentrate on everyday matters and the clarity of mind to see situations as they truly are, increased peacefulness, acceptance of oneself, an increasing awareness of the illusory nature of thoughts.

Loving 'oneself' should be viewed as an act of enlightened self-interest, not as mere selfishness.

**Tong-Len Meditation (Taking and Giving)**
This meditation is from the Tibetan-Buddhist tradition and engenders compassion by means of taking the suffering of others and replacing it with the gift of our own happiness. The practice concentrates on the specific nature of the thoughts we have in relation to other people. They can cause us distress of the mind, distress of the emotions and distress of the body. It helps to develop kindness to oneself and others, and as a side benefit, a more relaxed and healthy body.

Why do we want to do this? Primarily to relieve our own pain and suffering often caused by the confusion of not knowing who we really are. It may be helpful to establish that our first need is to find a way of understanding or transforming our own pain and suffering, then to have the intention of helping to relieve the suffering of others. If we are already dedicated to this viewpoint but have not attended to our own needs, it is essential to remember that to give love or help to others we have to receive it ourselves, otherwise it is an empty gesture – a bankrupt cannot give generously of money he/she has not got. When we truly receive and allow ourselves to be filled with love the experience can be so fulfilling that it spontaneously produces the wish to share that feeling with others. This effortless generosity is the fruit of such a practice.

**Step One: Meditation on Giving & Receiving**
*(for understanding and healing relationships between oneself and others)*
You've chosen an environment to do your practice. You're sitting in the comfortable posture of your choice. You also choose your motivation, i.e. maybe you want to relieve your own suffering.

Now you choose an embodiment of unconditional, pure compassionate love. In whatever form you perceive God, or the Universal Spirit, use this image to inspire your source of unconditional love, e.g. the forgiveness of Christ's love, the mother energy of the Virgin Mary, Tara, Shakti, Wakan Tanka (The Great Mystery) of the Native American tradition, or concentrate on the benefits of universal energy, the Mysterious Tao, or remember with gratitude how we are provided with support from our Universe i.e. food, clothing, shelter, friends, relatives etc. If these fail to inspire, bring to mind the qualities of a living or historical role model, e.g. the benevolence of Mother Teresa, Florence Nightingale, Gandhi, H.H. the Dalai Lama, or other religious or spiritual leaders.

As an alternative, consider more local or community-based personalities. Closer still, what about your grandparents, a favourite uncle or aunt or loving or inspirational friends. If that loving connection is not with an individual but an environmental situation (a beach or forest, etc.) then imagine yourself sitting in that nourishing and inspiring setting.

Another suggestion is to look for a time in our lives when we felt loved and cherished by someone near to us and recognize that the capacity for receiving that love is within.

**Healing practice**
Imagine the presence of the loving energy. On the in-breath, visualize or feel this energy centering into your heart. This can be in whatever form you feel comfortable, i.e. golden, white or rainbow light, or simply a feeling of warmth and compassion for oneself.

Allow it to mix with any physical pain or mental or emotional negativity from which you would like to be free. Discharge this in the form of toxic smoke on the out-breath. If you find this difficult to visualize, then concentrate on the feeling of relief or release.

If you feel you cannot visualize easily, bring to mind the idea of biting into a lemon and see if this produces an increase of saliva flow. Alternatively, imagine the sound of fingernails screeching down a blackboard!

Continue in this way, receiving love and releasing any negativity, doubts or fears until such a time as there appears little or no difference between the in-breath and the out-breath. It isn't necessary to emphasize the physical mechanics of breathing This could lead to hyperventilation taken to extremes. Conversely, it is quite common to find oneself spontaneously releasing mental, emotional or physical tension in the form of a deep sigh or involuntary body movements. As always, allow what is natural to occur without any form of judgement or restriction which, in itself, is a

45

way of ensuring a state of equilibrium.

Step One can constitute a complete practice in its own right, for the inability to receive love is a common form of imbalance in today's society. This may therefore be a helpful and simple way of practising healing for ourselves. How often have we been moved by the news of some disaster and felt powerless to help other than, possibly, on a financial level, thus doing little to diminish our own distress. An extension of this technique can be a helpful and simple way of sending healing energy to those we are concerned about, either on a personal level or in a wider context.

The following simple meditation can be an alternative or addition to Tong-Len at this stage.

### Meditation on Kindness (Metta Bhavana)

As long as you can breathe, you can do this practice. It does not involve elaborate preparation or complex mental gymnastics!

**Breathing in:** Being energized.
**Breathing out:** Wishing others well.

### Step Two: Tong-Len Meditation
*(for understanding and healing relationships between ourselves and others)*

It can be observed, in our day to day life, that we have a basic way of relating to people, objects and circumstances which we could define as principle forms of reaction. We judge things or people to be either 'good' or 'bad' in relation to ourselves. That which we deem unimportant we view with indifference. By using this practice, it is possible to see the 'relative' nature of this view and how it appears to be the root cause of all our suffering. For instance, we have all had an experience of being deeply attracted to an individual, even falling in love and, at some later date, disliking or hating them with equal intensity. The very qualities we initially found attractive are often the source of subsequent irritation. So let us examine the basic wishes of all living beings. We wish to be happy and free from suffering. We also wish to be loved unconditionally, free from judgement and limitation. In other words, to be accepted as we are. This meditational practice enables us to recognize this need in ourselves (Step One), and others (Step Two). This can purify many negative emotions and prejudices based on race, class, money, status etc., when we recognize our basic similarities instead of our differences. An excellent form of inter-cultural healing.

### The practice

Choose three people who are the following:

a) someone you love
b) someone to whom you are indifferent
c) someone you dislike

### a) Someone you love

Visualize, or bring to mind, the person you have chosen and recognize that they are no different from you in that you both need love and freedom from suffering. Imagine that their suffering and pain are in the form of a toxic or smokey cloud around them, obscuring your view. As you view them with sympathy and compassion, formulate the wish to take it from them and replace it with your own happiness.

**Technique:** On the in-breath, breathe this dark energy into your own heart, mix it and transform it into pure energy and on the out-breath return it to your loved one as loving compassion. Continue with this practice until they appear smiling and happy. This is an unconditional gift from you to the person you love with no strings attached other than their health and well-being. This is a way to purify possessive or selfish love. This is true compassion!

### b) Someone to whom you are indifferent

Select a person you do not know personally, e.g. someone you might have seen passing in the street or on the TV news. This person should be someone who has neither harmed nor pleased you. Follow the same procedures as outlined in the previous technique. They are no different from yourself or the person you love. This will be a unexpected gift to them.

### c) Someone you dislike

Initially, select a person that you 'dislike' rather than hate, in order to build the practice up in easy steps. (This is really practising compassion on yourself!) A person towards whom you have an aversion is someone you have 'judged' to be unacceptable in your world and you are attempting to push them away or deny their existence. By selecting them for your practice you are allowing yourself to dispense with judgement and respect their right to be who they are. In other words, you are extending to them the unconditional acceptance you would wish for yourself. 'Re-spect' can be regarded as 'having a chance to look again'. Repeat the technique of taking their unhappiness and giving them your happiness in return.

You may well think this is the most difficult part of the practice. However, compare this with the pain of letting go of someone you love. There are usually only a very few people we passionately love or hate because these emotions take up so much energy. In comparison, how many countless billions are there that we have not even thought about and to whose suffering we are indifferent. We will never be short of people on whom to focus this practice! This can be a way of transmuting or transforming our 'passion' into 'compassion' and become more loving and peaceful as a result of our understanding and commitment to change.

Our understanding is that we are no different from others. What we wish to receive as unconditional love, we practise giving. What we wish to give, we practise receiving. There is no difference. The balance between the two brings peace and equanimity. As our indifference to suffering (in ourselves and others) diminishes, our ability to grow with love and awareness increases.

This practice enables us to clear up the emotional pollution that clouds our relationships and brings us clarity of mind. Peace of mind reduces mental and physical tension and heals the conflict within ourselves. In the early stages we are removing the emotions we project onto others, creating a space for something else to happen. We are acknowledging that we are creating our own suffering in the way that we relate to other beings and that we have the capacity to change. We then have the choice between being overwhelmed by our emotions or transmuting them into a healing, connecting energy.

One way of coping with strong or unpleasant emotions is to discharge them. With Tong-Len, however, we can transform them from exhausting, destructive energy, to a force we can actually use. Taking an alternative view of human or animal waste products, a farmer or gardener can transform a substance viewed as 'bad' into compost (viewed as 'good'). In the East, this process is regarded as using the transforming power of the emotions as fuel for enlightenment. In other words, we no longer need to be frightened or distressed by the strength of our 'negative' emotions.

### Step Three: Tong-Len Meditation
*(having compassion on oneself)*

In order to prevent any unconscious retention of negative energies, return to Step One where you, once again, have an opportunity to receive unconditional love from your original source. This is a form of protection. As Shantideva says:

*"Whoever wishes to quickly afford protection to both himself and others should practise that holy secret: the exchanging of self for others."*

The meditation can be concluded by dedicating the results or 'merit' of the practice 'for the benefit of all (sentient) beings'. This unselfish dedication emphasizes our understanding that there is no difference between us and 'others'. Eventually you may even be able to thank those you were angry with for inspiring you to engage in your own healing process.

Many stories abound in Tibet of people with incurable diseases, i.e. leprosy, who adopted this practice to prepare themselves for death. To the astonishment of friends, family and themselves, they returned home after diligent practice, cured of their physical infirmities!

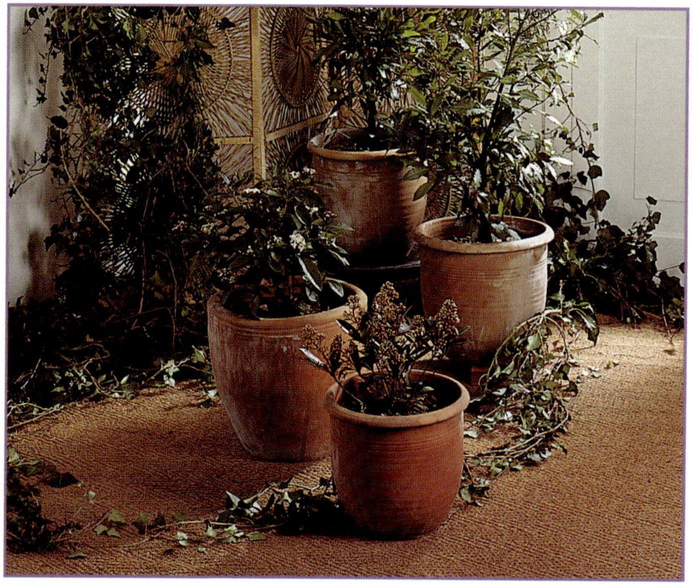